D0840899

CHRISTIAN NATURALISM

CHRISTIAN NATURALISM

Christian Thinking for Living in This World Only

KARL E. PETERS

WIPF & STOCK · Eugene, Oregon

CHRISTIAN NATURALISM
Christian Thinking for Living in This World Only

Wipf & Stock
An Imprint of Wipf and Stock Publishers
199 W. 8th Ave., Suite 3
Eugene, OR 97401

www.wipfandstock.com

PAPERBACK ISBN: 978-1-6667-3637-3
HARDCOVER ISBN: 978-1-6667-9457-1
EBOOK ISBN: 978-1-6667-9458-8

06/06/22

For Marj, in appreciation
for her listening love

A naturalistic Christianity is an event Christianity, a doing
Christianity, that embodies in its beliefs and practices the
universalizing of acting lovingly, which is the genius of Jesus.

Contents

LIST OF FIGURES

CHAPTER 5: WHAT DID JESUS DO?

CHAPTER 7: PRACTICING CHRISTIANITY

CHAPTER 8: INTO THE WORLD

INTRODUCTION:
WHAT THIS BOOK IS ABOUT

I'D LIKE TO REFLECT with you about what Christianity might look like if we assumed that we had only one life—this life here and now? If we assumed that there is no reality beyond the world as revealed by our own sense experience refined by science? If we assumed that there is no life after our current lives as individual, self-conscious persons? In other words, what would a Christianity look like if it were not supernatural but fully natural—a naturalistic Christianity? My hope is that I can lead you to understand this point of view.

This book is intentionally written for a general audience, even those who do not have much experience considering our questions. The style of writing I have chosen attempts to involve you in my own process of discovery. For example, in chapter 3 I will invite you to join me in assuming a first-person point of view as we begin our cosmic journey as hydrogen atoms 13.8 billion years ago. Our journey will involve us in the birth, death, and rebirth of stars, and it will portray our biological evolution in relation to all things changing on planet earth. Our journey also will suggest historically how human evil arises, how Jesus leads us in responding to evil, and what we can do to address human evil by loving God, our neighbor, and ourselves. All this will be developed with some of the most recent ideas from science integrated with ideas from Christianity, often in the context of my own life. You may wish to use your own experiences in place of mine.

There are two caveats I want to make. First, much of this book is based directly on science, and science is an ongoing process of discovery in many areas of life and the world. Some new discoveries may lead me to alter some of what I present. However, I have tried as much as possible to base my thinking on the best current science that I know. The second caveat is that I myself am not a scientist. I am a philosopher of religion who for over fifty years has tried to engage the best science of the day. I have been helped in this regard by scientists who are members or friends of the Institute on Religion in an Age of Science. Some of them have read and checked what I have written here. Still, I do not practice science but always am "looking through a window" at what professional scientists are doing. I hope I am not distorting what I observe.

WHAT QUESTIONS WILL WE BE CONSIDERING?

The topics we'll be discussing in this book are (1) creation, (2) God, (3) humanity, (4) evil or sin, (5) Jesus—what did he do to save humans from evil? (6) Jesus—who was he? (7) how we should follow Jesus in practicing Christianity, and (8) what happens when we die?

In the first chapter we'll sketch how our most general views of creation, of the world or cosmos, have changed from biblical times two thousand years ago, to the Middle Ages about one thousand years ago, and then to today. We will see that in each time period the worldview makes sense based on careful observation and subsequent reasoning. I'll ask you to join me in imagining what the total cosmos would look like if we were first-century Christians; then fourteenth-century Christians seeing the universe in terms of Dante's divine comedy; and finally, Christians of the twenty-first century accepting the worldview of modern science.

In chapter 2, in light of our two-thousand-year historical journey in chapter 1, we will see that the way most of us have thought about God simply doesn't make sense. If you are like me, having thought about God as a personal being when I was growing up, I think you will find that this doesn't work anymore. So, how can we think about God, the creator of the universe? After briefly examining ways different people throughout history have thought about the ultimate source(s) of all things, I'll suggest that, instead of thinking about God as a being who creates the world, we try thinking about God as creativity—as the creativity ever present in a vast, evolving universe. One way some religious thinkers have put this is: the word "God" is not a noun; "God" is a verb.

In chapter 3 we'll imagine our own individual creation beginning about 13.8 billion years ago, three hundred thousand years after the big bang. Using the first-person singular, I'll sketch how *each of us* began as a single hydrogen atom, continued to be formed in the massive explosions of very large stars, and in the evolution of life on earth from simple molecules up to the present. The take-home message from this journey is that each and everything existing today is related to everything else. We are all family.

In chapter 4 we will sketch our human evolution from early tribal societies in Africa until the present, paying special attention to the evolution of human morality and also to why immorality happens. In particular I will discuss from a historical and evolutionary perspective some roots of systemic sexism, racism, and speciesism (climate change).

In chapter 5 we will focus on the heart of Christianity, on Jesus as one who leads people to salvation from evil and to union with God. The key term for this is "atonement." Think of it as "at-one-ment"—united with God. Throughout Christian history there have been many theories or ways of understanding atonement. We'll consider and evaluate two of the most prominent theories, the "substitutionary theory" (Jesus on the cross was a substitute sacrifice for our sins) and the "moral exemplar theory" (Jesus was an inspiring example of how his followers should live).

In chapter 6 we will look at who Jesus was, including how he was born. Following some current biblical and historical scholarship, and operating within the framework of naturalism, I'll suggest that Jesus was conceived when Mary was raped by a Roman soldier. Although controversial, such an idea may help us understand the conflict between Jesus and the domination system of the Roman empire. In Palestine the Roman system includes the priests and scribes in Jerusalem.

Chapters 7 and 8 will focus on what it means to follow Jesus as the moral example of the way to overcome evil. Using the parable of the good Samaritan and the two great commandments, I will discuss what it means to love ourselves, our neighbors, and God. I'll develop the idea that each of us is a complex person with multiple sub-personalities, that we are internal family-like systems. Forms of meditation enhance loving ourselves as complex persons. Then I'll apply the systems approach to loving our human and nonhuman neighbors in local churches and in the wider world.

In chapter 8 I will explore ways of following Jesus into the world as we respond to evil—to systems of sexism, racism, and speciesism. Speciesism is discrimination against animals and other species based on the idea of human superiority.[1] It is humans using other species only as resources for human benefit and not valuing them for what they are in and of themselves. It means that we do not take into our "hearts" that earth in all its complex evolutionary interactions should be considered and respected foremost as *source*—the evolving source of all existence on earth.[2] I'll suggest that following Jesus into the world can mean following those who don't consider

---

1. See *Merriam-Webster*, s.v. "speciesism."

2. See Rolston, *Environmental Ethics*, 197–98.

themselves Christian but who nonetheless express Jesus's kind love to all people, all species, and their planetary environments.

Finally, chapter 9 will suggest that the ideas of afterlife and of heaven and hell are ways of preserving hope for just rewards and punishments when these are not forthcoming in this life. However, such an afterlife does not fit into the framework of a Christian naturalism. So, I'll close with the idea of a communal sense of just-love that followers of Jesus are called to fulfill in the ongoing lives of people, other creatures, and the planet itself. I call this point of view "social reincarnation" or "societal life after death."

HOW DID I COME TO ASK SUCH QUESTIONS?

My own religious roots go down deep into Christianity. I grew up in a liberal Christian home and in the First Presbyterian Church in Fond du Lac, Wisconsin. Beginning when I was in church kindergarten, I was actively involved all the way through high school. A special experience at our church camp when I was seventeen called me into Christian ministry. I went "under care" of Winnebago Presbytery, the church district of northeast and central Wisconsin. Being under care meant that I had a religious home base of ministers and lay leaders who followed my education through college and seminary until I was eligible to be an ordained minister in the Presbyterian denomination.

I never was ordained. Instead, I completed my PhD in philosophy of religion in the Joint Program of Columbia University and Union Theological Seminary in New York City. For the next thirty years I taught undergraduates in a wide variety of courses ranging from Asian religions, contemporary issues in religion and science, ethics, environmental ethics, and religious and philosophical issues in medicine. And every year I was responsible for teaching courses in Christianity: New Testament, history of Christian thought, and varieties of contemporary Christian theology. Now in my eighties, I enjoy how much this religious heritage has become encoded in the neurons of my brain, so that I can daydream with my own deep-rooted Christianity, asking questions like those above.

My roots also go down deep into another heritage, that of secular culture based on science and technology. My father was a mechanical engineer who designed milk-processing and cheese-making equipment for small cross-roads factories in rural Wisconsin, and later for large companies like Kraft. I saw firsthand his design drawings and went with him during the summers when I was an elementary school boy to observe how he applied his ideas to the layouts of the factories of local cheese makers.

The public schools in Fond du Lac gave me a fine education in English, German, literature, social studies, and also in mathematics, chemistry, and physics. Nothing was taught about religion. That was the educational sphere of the city's churches.

When I went to Carroll College, a Presbyterian school just west of Milwaukee, the required courses were in English, history, science, and social science. All other courses were electives, including courses in religion and philosophy. I majored in English and in philosophy. It wasn't until I entered McCormick seminary in Chicago, when I was twenty-two, that the study of Christianity, both academic and applied to ministry, became the dominant part of my life. I enjoyed and excelled in my courses, graduating first in my class.

By the end of my seminary education I had decided that I did not want to go into church ministry. I hoped to become a college teacher, which would require further education ending with a PhD. However, before entering graduate school I was able to participate in a special exchange program between McCormick and a German educational group. My wife, Carol, and I spent fifteen months in Germany. We attended the University of Tübingen. Carol attended courses in art history while I enrolled in Protestant and Catholic theology.

At Tübingen I had an "awaking experience" that changed the focus of my professional life. The experience occurred when I attended lectures by the Roman Catholic theologian Hans Küng. In November 1964 I was sitting at one of the bench-like desks in a large lecture hall at the university. During my senior year at McCormick, I had become interested in the ecumenical movement, in the dialogue between Roman Catholic and Protestant theology. It was the time of the second Vatican Council; change was in the air. Küng was a good choice for me, but when I was in Tübingen the only course he taught was on the sacraments—not something I was very excited about.

However, the way he taught this course changed the way I approached my own theology. Taking each of the seven Catholic sacraments, he examined what all the various sources said: Bible, church fathers, church councils, various theologians up to the twentieth century—including Luther and other Protestant theologians. Then, after considering all these sources as data, he formulated with reasons his own position. *His own position!* I remember thinking, "He's the first honest theologian I've ever met!"

This changed my life. I began to ask, "If I'm honest with myself, after all I have learned, what do I *really* think theologically?" Most of the Protestant theology I had studied in seminary originated with thinkers from Europe—especially Karl Barth, Emil Brunner, and Paul Tillich. They were outstanding thinkers. But when I began to think for myself, I wondered what a theology might be like if it were grounded in American thought and practice, in the contemporary natural and human sciences and their application to human living. This was what had taken hold of my mind when in 1965 I enrolled in the PhD joint graduate studies program of Union Seminary and Columbia University. As I worked for the next six years to earn my PhD, I began to ask whether theology could be constructed within the naturalistic worldview of modern science.

1

CHANGING WORLDVIEWS

The words cosmology and *theology* are fancy terms for how we think (*logos*) about the universe (*cosmos*) and how we think about God (*theos*). In her book *A God That Could Be Real*, Nancy Abrams helps us see how changes in our thinking about the universe affect how we think about God.[1] The problem is that, while our view of the universe has changed dramatically from the time of Jesus, our view of God has not. There is a disconnect between cosmology and theology, and this disconnect is one important reason why many Christians leave the churches that preach an old, outmoded theology. To understand this fundamental problem, we will first take a look at how cosmology, our view of the universe, has changed. We will jump from the first-century CE biblical worldview to the "Middle Ages" and the worldview of Dante's *Divine Comedy*, and then to the rise of modern science, ending in the twenty-first century with a naturalistic worldview. After this tour of three different cosmologies, we will consider how our thinking about God must change.

FIRST CENTURY—THE BIBLICAL WORLDVIEW

When you and I look up at the sky on a sunny morning, we see the same vista that people have seen for thousands of years. The sky appears to be a dome covering the earth. The sun rises in the east and begins its day-long journey across the sky dome to the west. The sun rises, the sun sets; it moves

1. Abrams, *A God That Could Be Real.*

1

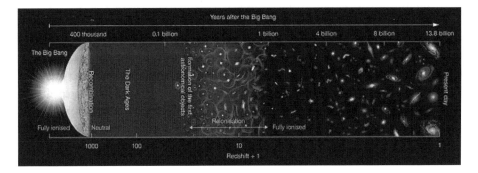

Fig. 4. Today's Expanding Universe. Credit: Argelander-Institut für Astronomie, Wikicommons.

Shapley believed that the Milky Way was the only galaxy; it was the universe. However, another astronomer in the 1920s, Edwin Hubble, thought there were numerous other galaxies. Today it is commonly said among astronomers that the universe is estimated to have two hundred billion galaxies, each on average with one hundred billion stars. We are awe struck.

Furthermore, Hubble was able to determine that all the galaxies in the universe were moving away from each other. He showed that the speed with which distant galaxies move away is proportional to their distance, which implies that the universe is expanding.

Imagine the surface of a balloon, blown up just a little so it is still small. With a Magic Marker we have covered the small balloon with black dots. Next, we blow up the balloon, and we see how all the dots are moving away from each other. This is the way it is with our universe. Looking at our balloon and recognizing that all the galaxies are moving away from each other, we come to another astounding conclusion. If we see everything moving away from each other, there must have been a time in the distant past when everything was together. So how did astronomers explain why everything is moving away from each other? In the 1940s, astronomer George Gamow concluded there must have been a "big bang" that created the expanding universe. This was confirmed in 1964 with the discovery of cosmic background radiation by Penzias and Wilson.[3]

---

3. Wall, "Cosmic Anniversary."

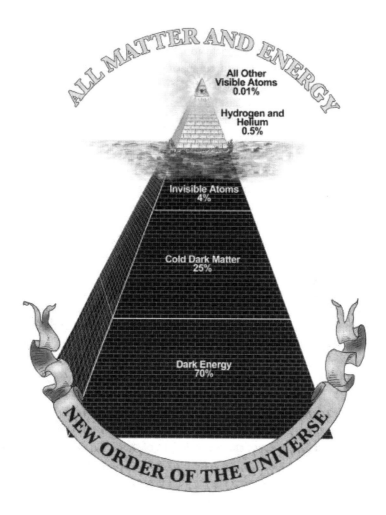

Fig. 5. Abrams and Primack, "Cosmic Density Pyramid." Permission from Abrams and Primack.

Today, in the twenty-first century, astronomers tell us that the big bang occurred 13.8 billion years ago. Oh my gosh! We have come a long way in two thousand years from the understanding of the universe in the Bible to today's understanding. We are overwhelmed.

Yet, there is even more. In the 1990s, only thirty years ago, astronomers came to the conclusion that all the stars in the universe are not everything that exists. They discovered that there must be something, some form of matter that cannot be seen, called dark matter. Dark matter is not south, the east, or the west. So where is God? In the biblical worldview of two thousand years ago God is "up there" as we point to the heavens. We can say that God is in the heaven of heavens. About a thousand years ago, with a Ptolemaic understanding, we can say that God is beyond the circling planets and beyond the stars.

However, the current scientific understanding is of an increasingly expanding universe that includes dark matter and dark energy. This gives us a "housing problem" for God—a major housing problem. Where can God and everything associated with God, such as "heaven," be located? How can we think about God meaningfully if we have a contemporary scientific worldview? We might begin by looking at some of the ways people have thought about God. A contemporary idea suggested by the twentieth-century theologian Paul Tillich is that, when we think about God, we are thinking about matters of "ultimate concern." What are our most fundamental concerns? Another theologian, one I wrote my doctoral thesis on, Henry Nelson Wieman, suggests that "God" refers to our ultimate commitments. What are we most committed to?

Whether we use the term *ultimate concern* or *ultimate commitment*, thinking about God means two things. First, if we ask how we spend our time, we can say God is that around which we organize our lives. God is the center of our existence. Seeking wealth in hedge fund management can be our God. So can a life commitment to human rights and social justice. Such things can be our most basic life concerns. However, in Western religious thought, God is not only the center of our lives; God is also understood to be the source of all existence. What is it that brings things into being—everything? One way of saying this is, "God is creator."

Activities such as seeking wealth or even social justice cannot easily be aligned with the idea of God as creator. So, the question has to be: can we think of God as creator of all things and at the same time as the center of our lives here and now? The following diagram presents some options as to how humans have thought about God as the center of our lives and/or the source of all existence.

GOD AS	Many	One
Personal	*Polytheism*: many deities of ancient cultures. E.g., the Greeks. Henotheism. Ancient Israel—Yahweh—no other gods before me.	*Monotheism*: Judaism, Islam, traditional Christianity. A universal God of all peoples.
Non-personal	*"Polyism"* [my term to compare with polytheism]. Various forces and laws according to which everything "runs." Forces of nature. Laws of nature. Possibilities for good.	*Monism*. Hindu—Brahman without form that gives rise to all forms of existence (including specific gods). Creative Process: (Henry Nelson Wieman, Karl E. Peters). "Unifying symbol for forces of nature and history that give rise to the human and make the human more humane" (Gordon Kaufman).

Another way of thinking about our options when we think about God is that God has been thought of as person, power (force), presence, process, possibilities, and principle in relation to our lives and the world as we know it—and also as mystery (transcendent) to indicate that all our ideas are only *just our ideas* about God.

Let's explore our options a little further by considering the notion *ultimate* or *sacred* (which is another word for *ultimate*, as I am using it). Audrey Shenandoah (1926–2012) was a clan mother of the Onondaga (a tribe of the Iroquois Confederacy). In an interview she tells Bill Moyers that, when she talks with children, she tries to help them understand what *sacred* means. She does this by asking what is the most important thing in their lives? They often will respond, "My mother." Shenandoah explains that this is because their mothers are the center of their lives. She then goes on to say that some Native Americans call the earth "mother." This is because the earth is the center of their existence, and their well-being depends on the earth.[1]

Some centers of people's existence might also be understood as the source of humans and other creatures. A Navajo story portrays how living beings originated in a migration of insects and other small animals up from the earth. These beings were transformed into the living creatures we see today. Humans can be regarded as one of these transformed beings.[2]

1. Moyers, "On the Sacredness of Mother Earth."
2. Long, *Alpha*, 44–53.

One creation story about the source of existence was most likely encountered by the Hebrews when they were exiled to Babylon (now Iraq) in 586 BCE. The Babylon story is about a feuding cosmic family. The ultimate matriarch of the story is Tiamat, the watery depths that is the source of all things and appears after creation in violent storms. Tiamat and her consort Apsu have offspring. When the children are young adults—teenagers—they enjoy a lot of partying. The noise they make disturbs Tiamat so much that she decides to kill all of them. One of the children, Ea, seeks a defender and finds among the third generation of gods, the grandchildren of Tiamat, a young warrior god—Marduk. Marduk becomes the champion that goes to battle against his grandmother—the watery depths from which all things emerge. Marduk, in the form of a powerful wind, blows Tiamat up like a cosmic balloon, pierces her with a spear, and defeats her. He then cuts her up and out of her parts creates the world that we know "today" in the biblical worldview. However, Tiamat is not completely destroyed; she returns in the storms and raging seas of our world. And resulting from his defeat of Tiamat, Marduk ascends to becomes the chief god of the Babylonians, who have conquered Israel.[3]

The Babylonian creation story is considered by biblical scholars to be one of the sources of the Genesis creation story. The word for the deep waters in the opening verses of Genesis, *tehom*, is a Hebrew cognate term for the Babylonian *Tiamat* (Gen 1:1–2). And throughout the Hebrew Bible and the Christian New Testament waters symbolize death and rebirth, for example, in the story of Noah and the flood, of Jonah and the whale, or in the Christian practice of baptism. There is dying by descent into the waters and then being raised up to be reborn.

The personification of natural forces may not be scientifically acceptable as an explanation of how things happen; however, personification can be a way for people to relate meaningfully to important aspects of the natural world. Let's look at the above chart again, especially the sections on the personal understandings of the divine as many and one. As I was growing up it was quite common for me to think of inanimate things in personal terms, especially if they involved motion. I personalized my Schwinn bicycle, naming it "Schwinny-Schwin-Schwinn." This enabled me to talk to my bike as together we rode the streets of Fond du Lac. I knew my bike would go faster if I talked to it. Of course, I did not think of my bicycle as a person but giving it a name established a personal relationship between the two of us.

Personal language may be a way of designating a relationship instead of describing what something is. God may not be a person but may still

---

3. Long, *Alpha*, 81–90.

be thought of as father/mother. Likewise, the evolving universe understood with mathematics is not a person from a scientific perspective. However, as the source of our human existence, our relationship to it can be understood in familial terms: astrophysicist Eric Chaisson says that we are "children of the universe."[4]

Likewise, we might imagine how easy it was for people like the ancient Babylonians to personify the forces of nature. After all, it's easy to talk about the vast, turbulent ocean depths in relation to us as the frustrated, violent mother Tiamat, long before modern science came to nonpersonal understandings of the forces of nature. Over thousands of years familial tribes, small nation states, and vast empires personified nature with their own names. Each community had people who created and told stories about gods and demons. And music, dancing, and chanting to these "beings" became ways of entering into relationships and interacting with them. The communities in the ancient Middle East were usually polytheistic, many gods often understood as being in familial relationships with one another.

However, the Hebrews were different. Having been liberated under the leadership of Moses from Egypt and given the commandments about how to live, their experience was of one single God. This god was their God. It's important to recognize that they did not deny the deities of other societies. However, these deities were not to be regarded as equal to or greater than the God of Moses. They were not to be worshipped—bowed down to. This is the meaning of the first of the Ten Commandments: "Thou shall have no other gods *before* me." In terms of our chart, this is called "henotheism," the worship of a single god without denying the existence of other divine beings.

Several hundred years after the time of Moses, some Israelites began to think that their god, Yahweh, or the Lord, was the god of all nations. There was only one personal divine being. Of course, this one, universal God—often but not always conceived as king—could have a heavenly court. How else does one make sense of the plural form in the creation narrative of Genesis, "Let *us* create humanity in *our* own image"? How else can one conclude that the serpent who speaks to Eve must be more than a snake? How else can we have angels such as Gabriel and Satan, the tempter, traversing between heaven and earth?

Monotheism (the belief that there is only one God) does not rule out other divine beings—we might say "spiritual" beings. Beings lesser than God, such as angels and demons. Not in Judaism, Christianity, nor Islam. And just as in polytheism and henotheism, these are understood as

4. Chaisson, *Cosmic Dawn*, 479.

and even the maintenance of galaxies, stars, planets, and life forms. Taking the argument to its logical extreme, we can identify the most dramatic and ongoing change—the expansion of the Universe—with the Prime Mover."[7]

That change—not permanence—is the hallmark of the really real is poetically conveyed by Nikos Kazantzakis in his *Report to Greco*.

> Blowing through heaven and earth, and in our hearts and the heart of every living thing is a gigantic breath—a great Cry— which we call God. Plant life wished to continue its motionless sleep next to stagnant waters, but the Cry leaped up within it and violently shook its roots: "Away, let go of the earth, walk!" . . . It shouted this way for thousands of eons; and lo! as a result of desire and struggle, life escaped the motionless tree and was liberated. . . . And lo! after thousands of eons man emerged, trembling on his still unsolid legs. . . . Man calls in despair, "Where can I go? I have reached the pinnacle, beyond is the abyss." And the Cry answers, "I am beyond." "Stand up!"[8]

Dramatically echoing Chaisson, Kazantzakis suggests that change and not permanence is the fundamental reality. This philosophical shift from permanence to change as fundamental to reality is, I think, the most significant shift in over two thousand years of Western philosophical thought.

A second shift in Western thought about the nature of reality is from thinking of each and every thing as a substance, separable from other substances, to considering everything as a system. A hydrogen atom is a stable system of a positive charge (proton) and a negative charge (electron). The only time hydrogen was created was near the beginning of our 13.8 billion-year-old universe. As the universe evolved other atoms were created, and hydrogen and other atoms combined into larger systems called molecules. Two atoms of hydrogen and one of oxygen combined to form H2O, a molecule of water. Water is a system. So are all other molecules. So are all those things composed of molecules, organisms for example. A cell on the back of my hand, or in the lining of my intestine, is a system. So are plants and animals composed of cells. My cat sleeping on the sofa on the other side of the room is a complex system within a larger system of me, our house, cat food, and cat toys. Human individuals are also systems—biological systems—that are nurtured by other earth systems such as rain, ground, plants, seeds, and animals. We are cultural systems—family systems, friendship systems, educational systems, and so on. Nothing is a hard-and-fast substance. Everything is a system composed of systems and existing in more comprehensive,

---

7. Chaisson, *Epic of Evolution*, 479.

8. Kazantzakis, *Report to Greco*, 291–92.

changing systems. Planet earth as a whole is a dynamic, extremely complex system, as we are learning from climate change.

Systems are not static; they are dynamic, constantly changing in the relationships between their parts and in their relationships with other systems. Interacting atoms, molecules, cells, organisms are constantly changing in relation to each other. We have returned to Chaisson's idea. The only thing that is permanent is change. *What is really real are dynamic systems.*

Let's use the idea of dynamic systems to reconfigure a basic Christian idea about God—namely, that God is Spirit. If one thinks of everything as substances, then God is a "spiritual substance." But what is a *spiritual* substance? In a scientific way of understanding things, how can one experience a spiritual substance? I suggest that the idea of God as "spiritual," so as to be experienced, can make sense in a relational understanding that sees things as dynamic systems.

In Genesis 1, the first phase of creation, the wind or spirit (*ruach*) of God moves over the waters, which represent a formless void. Spirit then also comes to mean that which animates or gives life. Like the wind, it can come to mean presences that are not seen but whose effectiveness can be felt in the world. Sometimes these presences are understood as forces or powers and at other times as personal, nonmaterial beings.[9]

Much traditional Western philosophy has thought of spirit in terms of nonmaterial substance. However, process and relational thinking suggest a different way of characterizing spirit and spirits—namely, as events or interactions. God as spirit is not understood as an invisible, nonmaterial substance. Rather, the idea of spirit refers to the interactions taking place as energy/matter evolves into more complex states of being.

One way to illustrate this is to look at the root meaning of spirit in the physical phenomenon of wind. In substantive thinking, wind is thought of as an entity in its own right that acts in our world. However, if one asks scientifically, "How does wind come about?" one discovers that it is the product of the interaction between high and low pressure systems. "Wind is caused by air flowing from high pressure to low pressure. The earth's rotation prevents that flow from being direct, but deflects it side to side (right in the northern hemisphere and left in the southern), so wind flows around the high and low pressure areas."[10] Differences in atmospheric pressure give us the experiences of the sounds and the visual phenomena (rustling leaves) associated with blowing winds.

9. See also Albright et al., *Interactive World, Interactive God.*
10. Coffey, "What Causes Wind?," para. 1.

In Genesis 1 the "wind" (spirit) of God disturbs the waters. In Genesis 2 God breaths into the sculpted inanimate clay the breath of life, and Adam becomes a living being. Wind and breath are the sources of change, the sources of life. However, from a scientific perspective they are not substances. Wind and breath are aspects of systems of dynamic relationships.

The idea of "spirit" as a system of dynamic interactions became clearer to me one Sunday when I gave up self-control and danced in church. Even I wondered, "Why does a seventy-three-year-old man start dancing in the aisle of a New England Protestant church? All by himself? Inviting others to join him?" My reply is that I was "moved by the Spirit."

The way I understand what happened is in the light of my scientifically informed theology that everything exists in dynamic relationships. Nothing is an isolated substance. Everything in the interrelated, evolving universe, from subatomic particles to world civilizations, is a dynamic system. So is the Spirit that moved me to dance.

One of the root meanings of "spirit" is wind—in Hebrew *ruach*, in Greek *pneuma*, in Latin *spiritus*. In ancient thought these words meant wind, breath, and soul, and they were conceived as substances. How do we understand wind today in light of what we know from science? Wind is not a substance but a flow of air molecules that results from the interaction of differences in atmospheric pressure. A few minutes ago, just before I started writing these sentences, the wind (spirit) whipped up in our yard. The people outside said, "What's happening?" Suddenly it turned cold, and air started flowing from the northwest instead of the southeast. A "cold front" had just passed through, the wind generated by the differences in atmospheric density between a low- and a high-pressure system, between warmer air moving clockwise and cooler air counterclockwise. This interaction produced a sudden blast of "spirit."

How does this relate to my dancing in church? As I experienced internally how this event began, I saw that it was the result of several other events happening together. The background event was that it was the fourth Sunday in the Christian season of Lent, and also St. Patrick's Day. It also was "spud Sunday" at South Congregational Church in Granby, Connecticut. On spud Sunday hundreds of potatoes are baked and put out on long tables with all kinds of toppings at the social hour after the service—a unique Sunday dinner of plenty in contrast to the Irish potato famine that brought many immigrants to America, including the ancestors of our senior minister, Denny Moon.

The Irish theme became a part of the service, with a fiddler and pianist playing Irish reels and jigs. The sermon Denny preached was the "Extravagant Gospel." It was based on the passage in the Gospel of John 12:1–8. Jesus and his disciples are in the home of Martha, Mary, and Lazarus on the out-skirts of Jerusalem. This is shortly before Jesus entered the city in the "Palm Sunday Procession." Denny focused on the interaction between Mary and Jesus, in which Mary broke several cultural boundaries by washing Jesus's feet with expensive perfume and drying them with her hair. The perfume was worth about a year's wages (Judas said it would have been better to sell it and give the money to the poor). The wastefulness broke rational economic boundaries. And by drying Jesus's feet with her hair, Mary broke the cultural boundary of that time between a man and a woman.

Fig. 6. Vedran, Cellist of Sarajevo, Ruins of National Library, CC BY-SA 3.0 view terms. File:Evstafiev-bosnia-cello.jpg. Created: 1 January 1992.

As Denny told this story he interrelated it with another story—that of Vedran playing his cello in the midst of the ruins of Sarajevo, which resulted from the brutal civil war. Thirty-three-year-old Vedran Smaliovic had played with the Sarajevo String Quartet and the Sarajevo Philharmonic Orchestra. He was devoted to the beauty of music. As his city lay in ruins, Vedran went out into the streets, the ruined buildings, and the cemeteries to bring beauty to the devastation. People asked, "Are you crazy?" He replied, "Who's crazy, me or those who destroyed our city?" Denny said that, like Mary, Vedran had broken the boundaries.

Mary's anointing of Jesus's feet with perfume was an extravagant act—beautiful but not practical. It appears to have been done in anticipation of

Jesus's death and burial. Vedran's music was extravagant good news that beauty could not be destroyed by war. Both actions—both interactions with their environment—broke the established boundaries. Both were examples of an extravagant gospel.

When the sermon ended, the offering was taken. Our fiddler and pianist played a rousing, upbeat Irish jig. And everyone *sat*—*just sat* in their pews, looking straight ahead, doing nothing. I thought to myself, "This isn't right." We have just heard a stirring, exciting message. Now we're listening to exciting music. And we just sit here, typical Protestant, Puritanical, New Englanders from the "land of steady habits." I could hardly stand it. A part of me wanted to move, to do something joyous. Another part—the cautious, rational man raised in the Midwest United States—was afraid of what was happening in his body, and of what people might think. A dynamic tension—like that between a high- and a low-pressure weather system—began to develop in my body-mind. I wanted to dance to the music, but I was held in place by my steadfast, rational form of religion.

I felt the pressure build as the lower part of my body began to move while I was still seated. Finally, I gave my body permission to take over. I allowed it to rise from my seat, move out to one of the side aisles of the church, turn to face my fellow congregants, and I let myself go—dancing to the music. Back and forth, side to side, in time with the music. I gestured to others to join me. Most just looked at me, startled. The three ministers up front looked—what was going on? Then they—Denny, Tamara, and Sandra—all rose up and started to dance. Denny came to the center aisle and danced up and down the aisle with his daughter. Up front behind the communion table, the choir began to sway. Some people in the pews got up and started clapping to the music, a woman joined me in our side aisle dancing with her little girl. The events of the day, the sermon, and the music—all interacted together as the Spirit of the extravagant gospel began to take hold—until the whole place "rocked." When it ended and I sat down, my wife, Marj, leaned over and whispered, "So this is what the 'emerging church' looks like."

After the offering, we sang our closing hymn, said our communal benediction, and sat for the postlude. Again, the fiddler and the pianist played an Irish jig, and the congregation rose up and swayed and clapped to the music. Inspired by the congregation, the musicians played on—and on and on and on—joyously. The congregation responded in kind, continuing to clap. Finally, the music ended. And the congregation erupted into a cheer. That day the Spirit—the dynamic interaction of Lent, St. Patrick's Day, spud Sunday, Mary washing Jesus's feet, Vedran the cellist of Sarajevo, and Irish music—came into the body of a seventy-three-year-old man, causing him to do something he had never done before, causing him to rise up and dance the extravagant gospel. He and others at South Congregational Church, Granby, Connecticut, felt "a blast of Holy Wind" uniting all in joy and love.

A SCIENTIFICALLY CREDIBLE IDEA OF GOD

God is not something other than the universe. Neither is God throughout the universe but more than the universe. Rather God is one way of understanding the universe. *God is understanding the universe as its creativity.*

What does our twentieth- and twenty-first-century cosmology do for theology? Simply put, if God is thought of as some kind of substance, some kind of being, the universe as understood by science creates a huge "housing problem for God." A God beyond an ever more rapidly expanding universe is no longer conceivable. Neither is God within the universe—if God is conceived of as some kind of substantive spiritual reality that exists alongside the physical world. The current scientific story of creation makes it impossible to locate God as a distinct reality within or separate from the world as known by today's science.

Yet, in a dynamic-relational understanding of things, it may be possible to think of *God* and *World* as *two ways of looking at the same thing.* Henry Nelson Wieman distinguishes between creative good or creativity and that which is created, created good.[11] In line with this, we can say that *creative* good signifies interactions among subatomic particles, atoms, molecules, and organisms that over time give rise to the emergence of new molecules and life forms. The emerged molecules and life forms are examples of *created* good. *Creative* good also signifies cultural interactions among people and existing social structures and patterns that lead to the emergence of new social institutions, ways of living, values, religious ideas and practices, and scientific understandings. These in turn are *created* goods.

However, creativity and its products are not separate. They are the same thing viewed in two different ways. As soon as stable forms (atomic, chemical, organic, social, and conceptual) are created, these interact with other created forms, and the interactions can give rise to more newly created forms. Created good becomes part of ongoing creative good. In a dynamic relational view of things, *World* in all its relatively stable manifestations becomes *God* the creative source of all things. And God is the World in its creative interacting.

Here's an example from the blog of philosopher-theologian Robert Corrington. It's about Robert Neville's "Great Ontological Creative Act." Corrington writes that Neville expresses this primal act as follows:

11. Wieman, *Source of Human Good.*

"Religion, I claim, is the human, symbolically enabled, engagement with ultimacy. The ontological creative act is arbitrary, gratuitous, undeserved, and surprising. How can we comport ourselves to this wild god, if you personify the ontological act?" Exit a personal god who is a being and who expresses human emotions and favors one tribe or nation over the others. Neville's god is extremely large, if we may use this spatial language in a metaphorical way. And the primal ontological act is not a once-and-for-all creation of the world, but an ongoing process. . . .

For Neville, and for me, there are breaks and disharmonies in nature. Neville states: "Here is where Corrington's Spinozistic distinction between nature naturing and nature natured is helpful." [This is similar to Wieman-Peters's idea of creative good and created good.] The ontological creative act can be viewed as nature naturing so long as the "nature" of nature naturing is nothing more than nature natured, that is the determinate world created. Nature naturing is the creating of nature natured.[12]

Reflecting on this passage from Corrington's blog, it can be asked: If God and World are really the same reality, why bother making the distinction at all? The distinction makes a practical (pragmatic) difference in how we live. When we consider the World, or created good, we have the tendency to want to preserve what has been created. When we consider God or creative good, we are open to and even welcome the possibilities of the as yet unknown, new, emerging good. For example, we live in a frightening era of climate change, the result of many kinds of human activity. If we focus on what has already been created and hope to preserve the rich and diverse world in which we now live, we will be seriously troubled by the destruction of habitats, the increasing rate of species extinction, and the increasing social turmoil as people migrate away from rising sea levels and from draught spreading across land masses around the world. We will try to preserve cities as they are inundated by flooding, develop more irrigation systems for crops in drought-stricken areas, and generally try to maintain our lives the way they have been. Losing created good is indeed significant—a global tragedy.

On the other hand, if we focus on creative good, we are reminded of how previous planetary changes, some with mass extinctions, led to the proliferation and flourishing of new species. Sixty-six million years ago, when the dinosaurs went extinct as the result of an asteroid colliding with the earth, a small rat-like mammal, the tree shrew, began to flourish and evolve, eventually leading to our own species. Of course, creativity does not "promise" the same good as before. Human living may be completely transformed.

12. Corrington, "Robert C. Neville," paras. 1, 3.

Something else may become dominant on the planet. But new good will emerge. Creative interactions will continue to work, bringing about things we can't foresee. It may even be a new form of ecological civilization in which humans and other species live in a more loving, just, and peaceful world. Or it may be the destruction of Vedran's Sarajevo—magnified millions of times. We really can't know. Our hope lies not in maintaining the status quo but in being open to new, yet unforeseen, good.

If God and World are two ways of looking at the same reality, then we can say that as the World evolves, so does God. As created good becomes part of further creativity, that creativity exhibits features related to the world at a particular time. An implication of this is that, before *Homo sapiens* evolved, the creativity of the world or universe—God—was non-personal. Further, in the continuing physical-chemical-biological aspects of the current world—on planet earth—God remains non-personal.[13] Creativity only becomes personal when human persons are involved. This means that before human persons, God is not intentional and does not know the consequences of actions. Thus, God is not responsible for evil. Evil itself is something constructed by and relevant only to humans. This eliminates the problem of theodicy: how can an all-good, all-knowing *being* allow evil as *he* creates and rules the universe? The answer is, in a scientific understanding there is no such being; there is only the non-personal creative process.

However, if God is understood as an evolving system of dynamic interactions that is creative, when creativity produces humans as created good that can intentionally and knowingly participate in creativity, then it becomes possible for humans to assign value to what creativity has done in the history of the universe and what it is doing now. Concepts of good and evil make sense when creativity evolves to its human form. So do concepts of salvation and of what humans must be "saved" from. So does an understanding of Jesus as "savior" who inspires people to realize in their lives justice and love.

13. Kaufman, *Theology for a Nuclear Age*, 52.

3

MY STORY, YOUR STORY

We are all connected.

—Denny Moon[1]

In chapter 2 I put forth the idea that everything is a system—systems that are created in the evolution of the universe and that become the active bases of further creation. In this chapter I will be using some findings from the sciences to suggest that, as systems, we humans are evolved of interconnected parts. As particular "whole" systems, we thrive because we are related in many ways to systems beyond us. Then I will develop the moral/religious implications of this interconnectedness.

I will be writing this chapter from the first-person singular point of view. The reason is that it is easier to make an extremely important point—namely, everything is interconnected, not in static systems but in systems that are constantly changing. So, as you read this story, it may help if you think about this as being your story as well. Imagine that you are the "I."

Telling the story from a first-person point of view was introduced to me several years ago by Jennifer Morgan in her trilogy of "children's" books, which also are excellent for adults. In this trilogy, illustrated by Dana Lynne Andersen, the first book, *Born with a Bang: The Universe Tells Our Cosmic Story*, the cosmos in the narrator. This first-person perspective continues

1. Denny Moon is the senior minister of South Congregational Church, Granby, Connecticut.

with *From Lava to Life*, and *Animals Who Morph*. I will do something similar, but in my imagination, I am telling my own story (and you are telling your story too) as part of this wondrous, evolving universe.

What am I? In some ways this is a strange question. The usual question is, "Who am I?" When I'm asked "who," I respond, "Karl Peters." This raises the following: "Who are you, Karl Peters?" Well, I was born eighty-two years ago in Fond du Lac, Wisconsin, an only son. I went to a liberal arts college, got married, and went to theological seminary. After the completion of my PhD in philosophy of religion, I taught at a liberal arts college. Now I'm retired.

ATOMS

But *what* am I? What am I made of? I weigh about 154 pounds and am comprised of seven billion billion billion atoms—that is seven followed by twenty-seven zeros. This is an unfathomably huge number. If I counted one number each second for sixteen hours a day, it would take about fifty years to count to one billion. I wonder how long it would take to count to seven billion, billion, billion?[2] And this is just me—and you. How many atoms in all living and nonliving things on earth?

My earthly body includes a variety of atoms and molecules. All are important, but I'm amazed that up to 60 percent of me is water. Every cell in my body is full of water. Our brains are 80 to 85 percent water.[3] Water can dissolve many substances, and this helps my cells to use valuable nutrients, minerals, and chemicals in their biological processes. The carbohydrates and proteins that my body use as food are metabolized and transported by water in the bloodstream throughout my body. Water also transports material out of my body.

HYDROGEN

Water is made of two atoms, hydrogen and oxygen. Where did the hydrogen and oxygen come from? I've learned that all the hydrogen atoms were formed about three hundred thousand years after the "big bang." This was my beginning, my birth—and the birth of you and everything else—all from the initial creative act, the incomprehensible inflation of incomprehensibly high energy. The initial inflation lasted only three seconds, and then the energy continued to expand, creating space-time. As the expansion of the

2. See Chaisson, *Epic of Evolution*, 2.
3. Sissons, "What Is the Average Percentage."

universe slowed down it became cool enough that protons and electrons could permanently fuse together. (When it was hotter, energy would blow them apart as soon as they were formed.) Hydrogen was created—and that is the *only time* hydrogen was created. All hydrogen atoms were created almost at the beginning of the universe. I, you, and everything else began as hydrogen atoms coming out of the initial inflation. Everything is 13.8 billion years old when all the hydrogen, some helium, and a tiny amount of lithium were created.

OXYGEN—STARS

In terms of the numbers of atoms, I am 24 percent oxygen. My oxygen was created in stars. Beginning about two hundred million years after the big bang, gravity began to pull "clumps" of hydrogen together until the friction between atoms was great enough that the atoms ignited. For most of my childhood as a star (like the sun we see now) I was fusing the hydrogen into helium. As I and my fellow hydrogen atoms did this together, we released tremendous energy, like a massive hydrogen bomb. At the end of our star-lifetime (which lasted about ten billion years), I and other stars with the same or greater mass than my sun, expanded and then contracted. Gravity pulled my hydrogen atoms so close together that they ignited and fused helium and other elements like carbon and oxygen. My sisters, more massive stars, could make even more elements all the way up to iron. That was when my life as a star ended. I died as I expelled much of the gas I had created into space. Because I was a sun-sized star, I expelled my gas gently. As I dissipated, I became a beautiful nebula.

The following image, taken by the Hubble Space Telescope, depicts the planetary nebula NGC 2440—an enormous cloud of gas cast off by a dying star. NGC 2440 is roughly four thousand light-years from earth, in the constellation Puppis. It is shaded to show different types of gas surrounding the star, which all glow differently due to their helium, oxygen, nitrogen, and hydrogen.

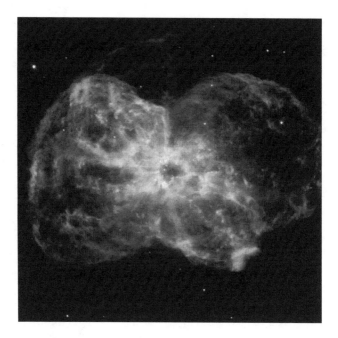

Fig. 7. Planetary Nebula 2440. Hubble Space Telescope, public domain.

The star is shedding its outer gas layers, which are slowly bleeding away into space. The gas glows due to ultraviolet light from the dying star. In the center, a white dot is visible; it's the remains of the star, called a white dwarf. There are many dying stars like this around the galaxy. Earth's sun will meet the same fate, but not for another five billion years.

SOLAR SYSTEM

My more massive star cousins ended their lives much more explosively, blasting out debris at almost the speed of light. They created atoms all the way to uranium. This mixture of elements was available to renew my life as a second-generation star—a star with planets. Here's how it happened.[4]

4. NASA Science, "Our Sun."

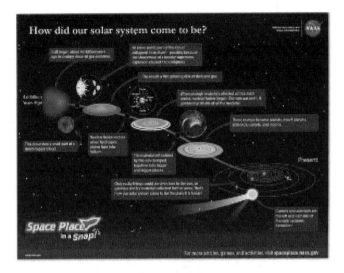

Fig. 8. Origin of Our Solar System. Space Place, Nasa.

About 4.6 billion years ago, there was a dense cloud of interstellar gas and dust—a planetary nebula, that had been created in my previous life as an exploding star. This cloud collapsed, possibly as a result of shock waves from a nearby exploding star, a supernova. When this dust cloud collapsed, I began a new life as a spinning, swirling disk of material, a solar nebula. As I spun gravity began pulling more and more material into the center of the disk, the same as when I became a previous generation star billions of years ago. I began to be born as a new star that would fuse hydrogen into helium for the next ten billion years. This star came to be called the "sun." But my birthing was not yet over. As the sun I eventually amassed 99.8 percent of the available matter in the disk. But the remaining two-tenths of a percent was itself quite large, and under the continuing influence of gravity it began clumping together. And the clumps smashed into one another, forming larger and larger objects—until (oh my goodness!) planets and moons of various sizes were created. I was astronomically reborn as planet earth along with my own moon. That was 4.6 billion years ago.

EMERGENCE

I began my cosmic biography saying that I was 60 percent water, and that water was composed of hydrogen and oxygen. But how did hydrogen and oxygen atoms, two gases, become a liquid molecule?

I remember this being demonstrated by my teacher in high school chemistry. He took a large tube made of nonbreakable glass and clamped it on a stand. The tube had a stop-cock on the bottom. Into the top of the tube he poured oxygen and hydrogen. Nothing happened. He lit a long match and touched the mixture. WHAM! A flash of light, an explosion. Then he opened the bottom of the tube, and out came drips of water. My teacher had demonstrated in our classroom what happens on a much larger scale as water is formed in the universe. Hydrogen + oxygen + energy forms water. Wondrous! Two gases combined to become a liquid.

According to cell biologist Ursula Goodenough this is an example of "emergence." She says that as anything—including you and me—moves up to larger levels of scale, one encounters "something else from nothing but." Importantly, this something else can, in turn, participate in generating a new something else at a different level of organization.[5]

The emergence of something else (something new and different) from simpler forms that come together "by chance," occurs throughout the evolution of the cosmos, life, and human culture on our planet. Here are some examples.

> From chemistry: when hydrochloric acid and sodium hydroxide combine, the result is salt and water, a product not at all consistent with the effects of either a strong acid or base.
>
> From neuroscience: consciousness is often called an emergent property of the human brain. No single neuron holds complex information like self-awareness, hope or pride. Nonetheless, the sum of countless neurons in the nervous system generates complex human emotions like fear and joy, none of which can be attributed to a single neuron. Most neurobiologists agree that complex interconnections among the parts give rise to qualities that belong only to the whole.
>
> From social science: complex human social organization also exhibits certain emergent properties. If a small group of individuals decides to create and locate a theater in part of a city with no cultural activities, similar activities nearby become more feasible. The group is joined by others who create art galleries, restaurants, museums, and schools. Gradually the area becomes a cultural district. No single person makes the

5. Goodenough, *Sacred Depths of Nature*, 27–29. A detailed discussion on "Emergence: Nature's Mode of Creativity" can be found in a symposium that occurred at a conference of the Institute on Religion in an Age of Science. Papers are published in *Zygon: Journal of Religion and Science*.

decision to generate a cultural center, but the confluence of separate individual interests creates the district through emergent properties.[6]

GOD AS SERENDIPITOUS CREATIVITY

In chapter 2 we considered that the term *God* can be used in a naturalistic worldview to mean "the creative process." Theologian Gordon Kaufman calls this process "serendipitous creativity," because prior elements in the process cannot predict what might occur in the future. His idea is very similar to the concept of emergence.

Serendipitous creativity points to dynamic and ever-changing systems, the parts of which work together in unpredictable ways to create such things as new life, new truth, and new community. In the birth and development of a single living human, various components come together in unpredictable ways to create a new individual. The interactions of our genes, our womb environment, our family environment, our wider society, and our natural world work together to make each of us a unique human being.

Serendipitous creativity is also a way of understanding how human communities are created. "Science is a human creation, but no individual at the time of its origins in the seventeenth century had any notion of the complex institutional structures, modes of education and discipline, moral and communal commitments, financial and physical resources, not to say ways of thinking which constitute science today."[7]

The same is the case with modern democratic governments. No one person simply thought out and produced the complex political systems we have today. Many individuals contributed to their evolution over time, but no one could have planned or predicted their contemporary manifestations.

It is the same with the building of cities. "Any modern city is the product of human planning and intention—every brick was laid by a deliberate human act, but no one simply decided modern London or New York or Tokyo would be a fine thing to build, worked out the plans, and then brought it into being."[8]

I have given a few examples of how all things are related. All things contain hydrogen atoms. Living organisms contain water. We have seen how new properties come about at various "levels" of existence. Now I'm

6. *Wikipedia*, s.v. "Arts District," last modified November 25, 2021, https://en.wikipedia.org/wiki/Arts_district.

7. Kaufman, *Theology for a Nuclear Age*, 40.

8. Kaufman, *Theology for a Nuclear Age*, 40–41.

suggesting that we live in a universe where something that is emergent is a novel result of serendipitous creativity—something else from nothing but.

THINGS RELATED IN EARTH-EVOLUTION

How all living things on earth are related is illustrated by this cladogram.[9] They (we) have evolved from a single source cell LUCA (the Last Universal Common Ancestor), indicated by the bottom vertical line at the base of the diagram. Humans are among the animals in the upper right.

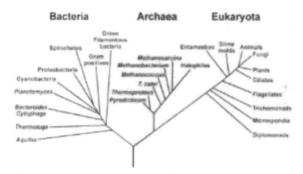

Fig. 9. Tree of All Life on Earth. Image by Eric Gaba, NASA Astrobiology Institute.

EARLY ATMOSPHERE

So how did you and I come into being on earth? We were born as the earth 4.5 billion years ago. By 3.8 billion years ago our atmosphere was primarily nitrogen, carbon dioxide, ammonia, and methane. It was not the kind of atmosphere you, I, and all our relatives could live in. It had no oxygen. What was able to live in this early atmosphere were some bacteria and other procaryotes, which had an enclosing membrane, often a flagellum for motion, and free-floating DNA but no nucleus of DNA.

9. A cladogram is a diagram that represents a hypothetical relationship between groups of organisms, including their common ancestors. The term "cladogram" comes from the Greek words *clados*, which means "branch," and *gramma*, which means "character." The diagram resembles the branches of a tree that extend outward from a trunk. See Helmenstine, "What Is a Cladogram?" Key aspects of a cladogram are the root, clades, and nodes. The root is initial ancestor that is common to all groups branching off from it. The clades are the branches that indicate related groups and their common ancestors. Nodes are the points that indicate the hypothetical ancestors.

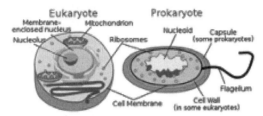

Fig. 10. Eukaryotic and Prokaryotic Cell. By Science Primer (National Center for Biotechnology Information). Vectorized by Mortadelo2005.

Then, about 2.4 billion years ago the "great oxygenation event" occurred. One of the bacteria was the cyanobacterium or blue-green algae, blue-green because it possessed chlorophyll. With chlorophyll it could convert carbon dioxide into oxygen. One billion years ago the earth's atmosphere became like the atmosphere you and I live in today.[10] The bacteria that lived in the earlier atmosphere went extinct as new kinds of creatures resulted from the universal creativity. These eukaryotes evolved into communities of cells that worked together and diversified through Darwinian natural selection into life as we now know it.

Fig. 11. My/Your Great . . . Great . . . Great Grandmother: Common Tree Shrew, wikipedia/commons/c/cd/Stavenn_Tupaia_glis_00., jpg.

10. "In some sense, when it comes to producing oxygen, cyanobacteria are the entire story. Because cyanobacteria can live anaerobically and aerobically, they are universally believed to have been responsible for the initial rise of atmospheric O2 around 2.3 billion years ago (Ga) (3, 4). Comparison of ribosomal RNA from cyanobacteria with portions of the DNA inside chloroplasts implies that all eukaryotes, including algae and higher plants, derived their photosynthetic capabilities from cyanobacteria by way of endosymbiosis (5). The Prochlorococcus spp. [species], an important component of today's marine ecosystem, may be the living ancestor of the cyanobacterium involved in this event (6). It appears that oxygenic photosynthesis—an extremely complex biochemical process—was 'invented' only once, and a primitive cyanobacterium was the organism responsible" (Kasting and Siefert, "Life and the Evolution," 1066).

My human history—yours too—a can be traced back to a small fury mammal who lived about 160 million years ago. (This mouse-like creature was "my/your great . . . great . . . great . . . grandmother.") We lived in the age of the dinosaurs. It was a difficult time. Imagine living and surviving in the midst of these huge reptile-like creatures. Most of the dinosaurs ate plants, but 35 percent were meat eaters. So, all of us smaller mammals had to be on guard. We weighed only about half an ounce, but we lived in trees or in burrows underground, hunted at night, and fed on plants, insects, and small lizards.[11]

Fig. 12. Asteroid 66 Million Years Ago. Image in public domain.

My survival was extremely important. You see, I was the first mammal with a placenta. I was the ancestor of all mammals with a placenta, "an organ that develops in a mother's uterus during pregnancy." The placenta attaches to the wall of the uterus and gives rise to the baby's umbilical cord. It provides oxygen and nutrients to a growing fetus and removes waste product from the baby's blood.[12] The placenta is a lifeline for species that evolved over the 160 million years. It's your and my lifeline too as we grew in our mother's womb from a fertilized egg into a kicking, screaming newborn infant.

Living in the age of the dinosaurs was always risky. Then everything suddenly changed. Boy, did it change! Sixty-six million years ago from the sky came a huge asteroid. It crashed on the west end of the Yucatan peninsula near Chicxulub, Mexico. It left behind a crater that spans ninety-three miles and goes twelve miles deep. It probably set a vast oil field on fire. The soot from the fire spread around the earth, blocking out the sun. The earth

11. Strauss, "Evolution of the First Mammals."
12. Mayo Clinic Staff, "Placenta."

cooled. Vegetation had a difficult time growing. In about ten years the asteroid annihilated the dinosaurs and obliterated about 75 percent of all plant and animal species on earth.[13]

TREE SHREW-DARWINIAN EVOLUTION

About four hundred thousand years after the mass extinction, I/you and other mammals began to evolve. Without those humongous dinosaurs, I more easily got food and other resources from my immediate environment, and reproduced myself with my opposite sex. I became part of a new phase of creativity, of ongoing creativity of all living things interacting with their environments. We were caught up in evolution by variation and selection—all natural. Usually, my created program of DNA did not adversely affect my ability to escape from those who wanted to eat me, my ability to digest food, my ability to have sex and produce offspring. So, I and my partner regularly birthed more tree shrews. However, every once in a while, my genetic program changed. Radiation, or a chemical I came in contact with, or simply an error when my DNA divided, changed my genetic code. This led to a change or changes in my body and behavior.

Often the changes did not matter much. Sometimes they were detrimental, perhaps affecting my eating or reproducing. But every once in a great, great, great while, a genetic change in my sex cells contributed to having a daughter tree shrew with a small change in body and behavior that increased success in reproducing. And with more success in reproducing a new, genetically modified tree shrew altered the course of the evolution of my species or contributed to the rise of an altogether new species. And the new species, through random variation and natural selection gave rise to still other species—until more than sixty million years after the asteroid crash and the great dinosaur extinction I/you emerged in the form of a human being.

BRICOLAGE

Even though you and I are each unique human beings, we have evolved with parts of us that are similar to those other animals. Through evolution no species is created from scratch. Already existing genes or other materials are adapted for new functions—bricolage. As Ursula Goodenough says, it's always "something else emerging from nothing but." Franz de Waal writes:

13. Siliezar, "Cataclysm."

"Evolution rarely throws out anything. Structures are transformed, modified, co-opted for other functions, or 'tweaked' in another direction—descent with modification, as Darwin called it. Thus, the frontal fins of fish became the front limbs of land animals, which over time turned into hoofs, paws, wings, *hands*, and flippers. Occasionally, a structure loses all function and becomes superfluous, but this is a gradual process."[14]

COMMON BODY PLAN, HOX GENES

A very interesting way about how you/I are related to other species is our general body plan, how we develop from "head to tail." In the species history of the earth, a body plan, once it emerges, evolves in a widely diverse number of species. The body plan is the result of homeobox genes or Hox genes. The amazing thing is that mammals including humans have Hox genes that are very much like the Hox genes of other creatures—even fruit flies. Yes, your and my body plan from head to tail is essentially the same as the plan of a fruit fly.

The group of genes known as homeobox (Hox) genes control embryonic development of the body plan in a wide range of animals, from humans and fruit flies to cats to beetles. These widely different animals, like many other familiar creatures, have bilateral symmetry, with similar left and right halves of a body laid out along a head-to-toe axis. During development, this axis is divided into a series of segments, and the Hox genes are well-known for determining what structure forms in each segment. They control where the head, shoulders, knees, and toes go; mutations in Hox genes famously result in body parts sprouting in the wrong place. Hox genes are highly conserved: "A Hox gene from a chicken can do its job just as well in a fruit fly, even though the two are separated by hundreds of millions years of evolution."[15]

OUR EARTHLY FAMILY TREE

The diagram shows part of our family tree that evolves from a bilaterally symmetrical ancestor. Every creature is a "close" relative. In the cosmic phase of our beginning, the common ancestor was hydrogen arising out the big bang—the creative act. Now 13.8 billion years later you and I are born as complex systems of living and self-reproducing cells. And we have a brain

14. De Waal, "Morally Evolved," 22.
15. Hudry et al., "Molecular Insights."

that can now realize that we are related to all other atoms, molecules, and living cells. We are all interconnected. We are emergent—a complex series of "something else from nothing but." We are one humongous cosmic family, mothered (fathered) by the bang.

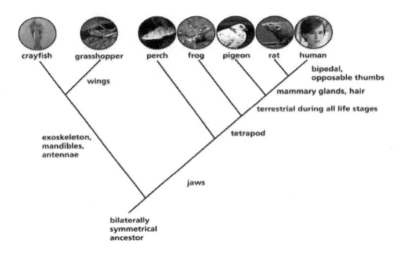

Fig. 13. Bilaterally Symmetrical Ancestors permission granted by the © 2021 Carolina Biological. Supply Company, 2700 York Road, Burlington, NC 27215-3398.

I can't help but think that I should treat all members of my family well, treat them like I would like to be treated. It took me 13.8 billion years to evolve to write these words. It also took 13.8 billion years for mosquitos, mice, coyotes, bears, daisies, tulips, and everything else to get to this place in space and point in time. This long history of coming into being in the present time makes everything valuable. That is why I can't kill anything unless it is absolutely necessary. I try to catch any critter in my house and put it outside—very satisfying to free a house fly that has been "trapped" buzzing at my large family-room window.

BRAIN EVOLUTION

Our most important feature as members of species *Homo sapiens* is our brain. Like the rest of us, our brain has an evolutionary history—as far back as the reptiles. About sixty million years ago we were mouselike creatures, scrambling around in bushes and trees. We especially liked the treetops— camouflage and tender leaves to eat. Our brains back then had evolved to keep us alive. They worked fast and automatically, especially when the other evolved creatures tried to attack and eat us. Our little reptilian brain responded to such threats with three instinctual possibilities: fight, flight, or freeze. These three automatic responses kept us alive long enough to reproduce. That was the name of the evolutionary game. Some of our cousins weren't so lucky; they lost, but as food they helped sustain other creatures.

As I've said, through evolution we came to be small mammals—like tree shrews. Nature uses things that have already been created in its new phases of creativity. So, when we came into being as tree shrews, we not only had the same brain as reptiles but also, integrated with our reptile brains, new parts in what is called the limbic system. We could experience "emotions." We could quickly and unconsciously experience and respond to the emotional states of our fellow creatures even as we were projecting our own emotions to others.

This allowed us and our evolutionary successors to be together in a community and together respond to food opportunities and to threats to our lives.

As you and I continued to evolve over millions of years, we became part of the primate lineage, which included our closest relatives, the chimpanzees and bonobos.[16]

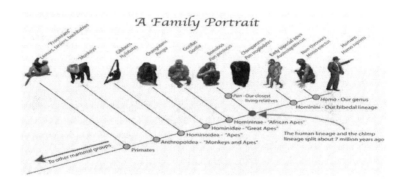

Fig. 14. Our Primate Family Tree, by Adam Pritchard and Matt Borths, Stony Brook University, NY. http://www.pasttime.org/2013/08/ episode-5-throwing-in-human-evolution/.

Each has a different kind of society. Chimpanzee societies are hierarchical, and each chimp band is usually ruled by a dominant male. We might say, when we are in our "chimp mode" of being, we are very much aware that our band can be in conflict with other chimp bands as we forage for food. When

16. "Our Primate Family Tree," http://www.pasttime.org/2013/08/episode-5-throwing -in-human-evolution/.

we encounter each other, there often is a fight, which can be quite brutal, with killing and maiming, until one band leaves the scene. And here is the irony. The band in which members cooperate together the best is likely to win the battle. Some think that cooperation in my group when we are in conflict with other groups is evidence of the rise of morality. Furthermore, conflict within a chimp society is resolved when the more powerful chimp, usually the patriarch, overcomes physically or psychologically those with lesser strength and power. Some human anthropologists call this the "warfare hypothesis" of morality.

Bonobo societies are different. If we were in a band of bonobos, the band would be governed by the females. Conflicts are resolved by females having sex with each other—what fun. Bonobo morality is based on enjoyable sexual relations that bind members of a bonobo band together in cooperative relationships. We see that the difference in the roots of morality or cooperative behavior is *power* vs. *love*. (This will be important later when we consider the love ethics of Jesus in relation to systems of domination.) I, you, and other humans probably have both biological roots in our reptilian-mammalian brains.

Then a truly remarkable thing happened. Over millions of years a new brain evolved—laid over the top and in front of, yet interconnected with, our lizard-mammal complex. Our new brain system, the neocortex, helps us speak words that other *Homo sapiens* can understand and then talk back to you and me. We can think abstractly and develop mathematics, create art and music, and imagine a future different from the present.

By imagining a different future, we can ask ourselves whether we want things to be different from, better than, the way they are now. And we can act in ways that help that better future come about. I and you began to develop a conscious sense of how things should be, not just how they are. What should we do when we effect how other things should be? What is right and wrong, good and bad? When are we good or do good, and when are we bad or do what is bad?

Most important, whose future should we be concerned about—just our own future, just the future of family and close friends, just the future our religious community, just the future of our present society, just the future of the entire human community, just the future of all sentient creatures, or the future of the entire planet earth. Questions regarding whose future should we be concerned about are questions about who is in the moral community. If we ask and try to answer, "Who is in the moral community?" we can find an evolutionary pathway to consider the question, "How is it that I, and you, and all other human beings became moral?" At the same time we find a related pathway about how we and others can also be immoral. In the following chapter, I will explore why we are both moral and immoral creatures—why we are morally "ambivalent" creatures. Wrestling with these questions provides a naturalistic way to consider what Christianity has called "sin."

4

HUMAN EVIL

A MAJOR THEME OF this book is that we are dynamic systems—related within as our own inner systems function well, and related externally to other dynamic systems such as families, local communities, nations, and even the entire planet. If we function well in relation to other well-functioning systems, we have a better chance to continue as a dynamic system.[1] I now suggest that this understanding leads to a way of formulating what is good and bad for us—for everyone and everything. As we contemplate what we should be doing to help create a future, behaviors of individuals or societies are good insofar as they help maintain well-functioning, existing systems throughout their life-times. In a dynamic world this also means supporting the creative process so that new systems of various kinds can emerge, so that new good is created. In the theology that I'm developing, supporting the creative process means being faithful to that universal creativity called God. So, being moral means both sustaining the well-being of already created dynamic systems and at the same time being open to creativity (God) and the emergence of new systems.

One way to express the norm of intentional morality and also of Christian faith is *(1) being a well-functioning system that (2) also engages to help maintain other created well-functioning systems and that (3) contributes to the creation and maintaining of new well-functioning systems.*[2] This chapter

---

1. Of course, we may encounter the slings and arrows of outrageous fortune. No one is immune to unforeseen events that can change our lives entirely. Remember what happened to the dinosaurs when a large asteroid collided with earth.

2. In chapter 8 we will see this expressed as loving oneself, loving one's neighbor as

will focus on things that prevent our being moral. In traditional Christian terms, we will be exploring how sin comes about.

In our evolutionary history there are many factors that have made us capable of being moral, immoral, and indifferent to the immorality that occurs around us. One of the most important factors underlying what makes us moral is *empathy*. According to neurologist Antonio Damasio, empathy is an "action program" that works below the level of conscious awareness.[3] Without our consciously realizing it, our brains pick up cues from other people and respond appropriately in supportive ways. Later in the history of brain evolution we also develop conscious inner feelings of what others feel.

Without empathy, we could not appropriately follow universal moral codes such as "do not do to others what you would not have them do to you," "do onto others as you would have them do unto you," and "love your neighbor as you love yourself." To follow such universal moral laws, we have to be aware of and feel what others need or do not need. If we cannot empathize with the needs of others, we may mistakenly project our own needs onto them. To love others as we love ourselves, we have to know what they need, not what we need.

At the end of the last chapter I sketched the evolution of our group of genetically related organisms. Let's continue our autobiography. This time we will remember the past from our twenty-first-century standpoint. Taking our current standpoint will make it easier to use scientific understandings from anthropology, genetics, neuroscience, and psychology to reflect on our past up to the present. This will help us gain a better understanding of how we became moral creatures and how we can become immoral.

As I trace your and my stories with the help of scientific findings, let's begin one hundred thousand years ago when we were humans in Africa. We lived on the shore of Lake Turkana in the great rift valley that divided Africa. Our valley was part of a series of rifts that ran from Mozambique in the southeast part of Africa, through the Red Sea and the Dead Sea, and up the Jordan Valley to eastern Lebanon.

oneself, and loving God with heart and soul and mind and strength.

3. Damasio, "Neural Basis of Emotions."

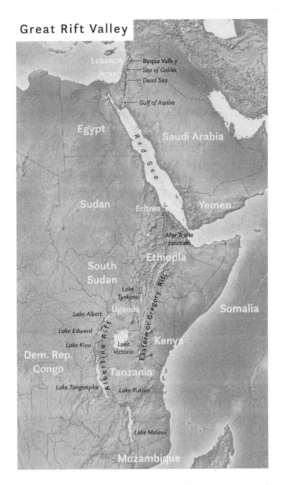

Fig. 15. Great Rift Valley in Africa, CC BY-SA 4.0File:MapGreatRiftValley.png,
Created: 24 March 2017, Map produced from scratch using public domain source
data by Redgeographics

You and I were infants in a tribe of hunter-gatherers, about fifty children, women, and men. We lived where lions, tigers, and crocodiles looked
at us for their dinner. And other human tribes competed with us for food
and natural space. Our being moral included all of us working together as
an integrated, dynamic system, in order to reproduce, survive, and flourish.

I and you were especially vulnerable. We were infants, newly born.
The future of our tribe depended on us growing up and having children
of our own. Fortunately, to our advantage, we had dark skin with enough
melanin to protect us from the sun. We also had very nurturing families.

Our mothers carried us with them for up to four years. Our fathers also carried us when we made long journeys to move our camps. We had aunts and uncles and cousins who watched out for us. This kind of extended family nurturing was the norm for thousands of years.

We began migrating out of Africa about one hundred thousand years ago up the Great Rift and across the lower end of the Red Sea. Then we went west along the north shore of the Red Sea, up past the Dead Sea, and along the Jordan River to Lebanon. Other tribes went East to India, Australia, China, and eventually reached the Americas about twelve thousand years ago.[4] Native Americans still had our tribal African form of child rearing until Euro-Americans conquered the natives, uprooting families and destroying much of the fabric of tribal civilization.

SYSTEMIC SEXISM BEGINNING WITH THE AGRICULTURAL REVOLUTION

A very important phase of the migration out of Africa was the settlement of an area called the "Fertile Crescent," sometimes called the cradle of civilization.[5] This map shows the location and extent of the Fertile Crescent, a region in the Middle East incorporating Ancient Egypt; the Levant; and Mesopotamia.

Fig. 16. Map of the Fertile Crescent, Nafsadh, CC BY-SA 4.0, Created: 22 May 2011.

4. Some scholars find evidence for multiple migrations from different parts of Africa. In this book we are following one possible migration.

5. Similar "civilizations" were occurring about the same time in the Indus River valley, the Yangtze River, and the Nile.

It was here that the rise of agriculture with the domestication of plants and animals began about 10,000 BCE. There was a transition from hunting and gathering to settled farming. The region had considerable variety in elevation, creating "microclimates." This supported the rise to many species of edible plants. The Fertile Crescent was home to eight "founder crops," the wild progenitors of emmer wheat, einkorn wheat, barley, flax, chick pea, lentil, and bitter vetch (a lentil-like crop for cows). It was also the origin of four of the five most important species of domesticated animals—cows, goats, sheep, and pigs.[6] The horse may have originated in North America. It migrated to Asia and Europe but then became extinct in North America about ten thousand years ago, only to be reintroduced from Europe.

Fig. 17. Ancient Farming. Wikicommons, History for kids.

So, we settled down to a sedentary lifestyle of farming and herding. This gave us a regular supply of high-calorie food. Our mothers, aunts, and other women were better nourished. Women did not have to go out to gather food like we had done for so many thousands of years. Mothers could stay at home with us kids. Because intervals between births decreased, you and I had more brothers and sisters, and also more cousins. We were part of a growth in population. We lived closer together in larger settlements than our tribes of long ago. Cities began to be built. This led to settlements, an increase of population density, the number of cities, and after a few thousand years the establishment of empires.

6. Diamond, *Guns, Germs, and Steel*, 480.

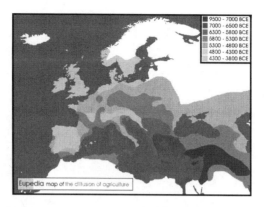

Fig. 18. Diffusion of Agriculture, GNU Free Documentation License, Version 1.2, November 2002, Copyright (C) 2000, 2001, 2002 Free Software Foundation, Inc. 51 Franklin St, Fifth Floor, Boston, MA 02110-1301 USA.

As our population grew there began a series of migrations. Most migrations were from the Fertile Crescent west to Anatolia (central Turkey) and then to what is now Europe. From Spain to northern Europe, these people settled down to farm and graze the land.

But you and I traveled in a group that went north along the shore of the Caspian Sea (see figure 18) with the high, rugged Caucasus Mountains to our west ending at the Black Sea. Finally, we reached the steppes of Russia and Ukraine. (The steppes are fertile grasslands for grazing, beginning in eastern Europe in the north and going all the way east to Mongolia.) We continued further north and finally settled on the steppes that formed the western edge of the Ural Mountains. We found ourselves among the Yamnaya. These people of the Russian and Ukrainian steppes rode domesticated wild horses. They also built wagons with wheels that could pulled by horses. For the first time ever we saw horses.

Fig. 19. Horses By Soghomon Matevosyan - Own work, CC BY-SA 4.0, https://
commons.wikimedia.org/w/index.php?curid=106833263.

The Yamnaya were a mobile herding society. They migrated long distances into India and northwestern China—and westward into Europe. About 3500 BCE we joined a Yamnaya migration that moved west along the Danube River into Europe. As we began our trip through southeastern Europe (what now is known as Moldova, Romania, and Bulgaria) we found artifacts from an earlier matriarchal society that worshipped female deities.[7] The earlier matriarchies had probably been conquered by earlier Yamnaya.

Fig. 20. Yamnaya, construction by Philip Edwin, Deviant Art Nov. 26, 2021.

7. See Gimbutas, *Living Goddesses*.

Continuing up the Danube into western Europe, we saw the impact of a plague that had reduced the populations of already existing hunter-gatherers and farmers. Conflict reduced the population even more, giving us an opportunity to be successful, helped by our new technology of wagons and our horses. We could more easily harvest grain from greater distances than earlier farmers, who could harvest only walking distance from their homes. Our herding of cattle, sheep, and goats provided increased nutrition for us. So our farms became larger in size as we outproduced the older inhabitants. We had few women with us, but we married the farm women who had survived the plague and fighting. In Iberia (or Spain), we replaced all the Y chromosomes of the Iberian men with Yamnaya male chromosomes.[8]

Fig. 21. Yamnaya Migration Up the Danube, Europe Copyright (C) 2000, 2001, 2002, Free Software Foundation, Inc.

8. About forty-five hundred years ago "nomads from the steppes of what is now Russia turned up in eastern Europe with horses and wagons. They spread across the continent, giving up nomadic life and intermarrying with European farmers. When they finally reached Iberia, these people spread out far and wide. 'They really have an impact on the whole peninsula,' said Dr. Olalde. But skeletal DNA from that period is striking and puzzling. Overall, Bronze Age Iberians traced 40 percent of their ancestry to the newcomers. DNA from the men, however, all traced back to the steppes. *The Y chromosomes from the previous male farmers disappeared from the gene pool*" (Zimmer, "History of the Iberian Peninsula," italics mine). In a review essay Arthur Krim says that "David Anthony has produced convincingly detailed evidence that plants the origins of Indo-European culture firmly on the Russian-Ukrainian steppes by 3500 BCE and demonstrates the spread of its horseback-riding innovations westward up the Danube River in Central Europe and eastward over the Iranian plateau into the Indus Valley." Krim, review of *The Horse*, 573.

Besides changing genes, we also changed how society was organized. Historically we had organized around small monogamous families and the individual ownership of animals and land.[9] In this way we contributed to the foundation for the formation of societies and how things would be for centuries to come. Furthermore, some think that we brought a new language that became the basis for four hundred languages called the Indo-European language family.[10]

Centuries later, the rise of a succession of middle eastern empires culminated with Rome. When Rome's political power declined, Christianity, which had become the religion of the empire during the reign of Constantine, emerged as both a religious and political driving force in Europe.[11]

PERSONAL EXAMPLES OF SEXISM

Reflecting on our journey out of Africa that ends in Europe, I believe it helps us see the early history of sexism. It seems that the most egalitarian societies occurred when we were still African hunter-gatherers. We remember that when we married, there was a choice where we would live. Either sex could live with the others family and most of the tasks could be shared.

However, after migrating to the Fertile Crescent, as the population grew, the social system became more complex. The tasks of living diversified. We begin to see the rise of hierarchies and of political leaders who are warriors and emperors. Young women would leave their families and settle down with their husbands in the midst of his coworkers and friends. Sara Blaffer Hrdy points out that with the rise of the "cow and plow" system of food production, the interest groups of men became more important and more ecologically feasible. Settled, patrilineal societies expanded at the expense of the more flexible and variable residence patterns characteristic of hunters and gathers.[12]

9. Faculty of Science, University of Copenhagen, "Steppe Migrant Thugs."

10. "The Yamnaya lifestyle appears to have been a mixture of pastoralism, agriculture, and hunting and gathering which is similar to the lifestyles of later European cultures such as the Celts and early Germanic cultures. This makes sense since these recent findings would suggest that the Germanic people and the Celts were their descendants" (Strom, "How a Handful").

11. As the Roman and Holy Roman empires spread through Europe, I can't help but wonder if the spread of the Y chromosome from the Yamnaya, introduced centuries earlier, might have played some biological role in the rebellious Protestant Reformation, the Thirty Years' War, the Spanish conquistadors, the Europeans conquering the Native Americans, the formation of multigenerational slavery, the European colonialization of the world, the twentieth century of wars, and yes, systemic sexism.

12. See Johnson, "Raising Darwin's Consciousness."

In the twenty-first century and the nuclear family, the focus of men's activity is the job. Women and children often move to live where the husband's job is located. This is certainly the case with my own family; it might be with yours. Even though my grandmother was qualified to be a school-teacher, when she married my grandfather early in the twentieth century, she moved from her home in the center of town to the outskirts and became a farmer's wife. Thirty years later, her daughter married my father and moved 120 miles away from her home to where my father worked. Even though mom had a bachelor's degree in English from the University of Wisconsin, she never used that degree. She became a housewife.

When my first wife, Carol, and I were married in 1961, during the summer after I graduated from college, she was already working in a large Chicago company as a system's engineer. I studied for the ministry in Chicago, for a PhD in New York, and in 1973 was hired to teach at Rollins College in Florida. Carol continued to work. Even though she had a substantially higher-paying job in New York as a systems engineer at IBM than I would have as a professor at Rollins, she always moved to where my schooling or job was and then sought work for herself. Even though she was the primary breadwinner in our family and managed our money exceptionally well, when it was time to move somewhere else, Carol followed in my footsteps. She was like most other women.

Then everything changed. One Friday she came home and angrily shouted, "I quit!" She went into our bedroom and slammed the door. She quit, and she never went back. For almost fifteen years she had worked for IBM. She was only a few months away from her vested retirement. And she quit—just like that.

It wasn't until sometime later that I learned why. Her new boss had hit on her! I wonder if this could have been the beginning of sexual harassment.

Systemic sexism is always present. It has been present in the structures of patriarchal societies ever since we moved out of Africa and settled down to become farmers and animal herders. It is present in all of us no matter what we consciously proclaim.

PROJECT IMPLICIT

Think for a minute. Do I/you participate in systemic sexism? In the society in which we live, a society of liberal, progressive, and Christian values, do I have parts that are in hidden but often emerge into consciousness when I'm discussing these topics with others or avoid going to discussions.

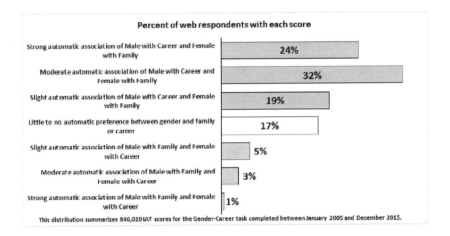

Fig. 22. Project Implicit Results of Gender-Career Task.
https://www.projectimplicit.net/

How intractable sexist, racist, and species-biased parts are is that we often are not even aware of them. They are hidden in our unconscious. This has been identified by some scientists as "implicit bias," bias against certain types of humans as well as certain types of life organisms. Mazarine Banaji and colleagues have discovered there are all kinds of these biases—biases against the elderly, the physically handicapped, provocative sex-related dress codes, dark skinned people, and certain kinds of animals. Banaji and her colleagues have developed a way of bringing unconscious biases or prejudices to light, even when people consciously deny them. It's called "Project Implicit."[13]

Project implicit is designed to measure a person's reaction times by rapidly and randomly presenting one each from two sets of terms. The terms below define male or female, and career or family. People who take the test are asked to decide very quickly whether or not the gender terms fit with the occupation terms. They do this by pushing the letter "E" or "I" on the computer. Their speed and accuracy in doing this determines a person's implicit attitude. The two sets of terms are male or female and career or family.[14]

Male   Ben, Paul, Daniel, John, Jeffrey

Female   Rebecca, Michelle, Emily, Julia, Anna

13. See the Project Implicit website, https://www.projectimplicit.net/.

14. There are several implicit-association tests. Among these are race (Black-White); transgender (transgender-cisgender); disability (disabled-abled); Arab-Muslim (Arab Muslim-other people); weapons (weapons–harmless objects); presidents (popularity); sexuality (gay-straight); weight (fat-thin); gender (science career–liberal arts career).

Career	Corporation, Salary, Office, Career, Professional, Management, Business
Family	Wedding, Marriage, Parents, Relatives, Family, Home, Children

> The results of the Implicit Association Gender-Career Tasks (846,202 scores from 2005 to 2015) show that there is a strong gender bias—suggesting that women are expected to be homemakers and men work outside the home. 56% show a strong or moderate automatic association of male with career and female with family. Only 6% show a strong or moderate association of male with family and female with career. It light of the history we have been outlining, this is not a surprise.

THE POWER DIFFERENTIAL

Underlying sexism and other forms of discrimination is a "power differential." Those in power have an advantage. And they often can use that advantage to fulfill their desires or goals by manipulating and discriminating against others. Genevieve Angelson is a star of the TV series *Good Girls Revolt*. The series is based on the true story of how a group of women in 1969 filed a claim against *News of the Week* (*Newsweek*). The claim was that the news magazine violated a recent federal law against discrimination in the workplace. The violation was that at *News of the Week* women could be "researchers" for male writers, who were "reporters," but women could not write the news articles and have their names in the byline. Sometimes the women were "ghost writers." This is all narrated in *The Good Girls Revolt: How the Women of Newsweek Sued Their Bosses and Changed the Workplace*. The author was one of the participants, Lynn Povich.

The star of the TV series is Genevieve Angelson. In a recent blog article, she explains how, when she was twenty-one, she said yes to a prominent, established film producer when he tried to make her his sex partner. After narrating how she became trapped, Angelson concludes her blog:

> I understand this now: sexual intimidation doesn't have to look like a bad man in his hotel room in order to intimidate. Intimidated, in a state of fight or flight, looking for the path of least resistance, for many of us that path is consent. We made a different choice to protect ourselves than the people who protected themselves by running out of a room. Like a well-behaved rabbit in the jaws of a wolf, rather than struggle, we went limp. I went limp.
>
> *If one is in a position of economic power over a "partner," can consent ever be clear, even to the consenter herself? How does either participant know if consent is made in fear?* The very archetype I

punished myself with—this intern with loose morals who sleeps her way to the top— . . . is a fiction that situates the locus of power in her. This femme fatale who somehow exudes the power to slay producers who outrank her in every single way—age, status, security, reputation, cohorts—doesn't acknowledge the reality. There is no such thing, there is no such woman. *What it looks like is this: a coercive, oppressive power imbalance in which saying yes is not the alternative to saying no. It is the alternative to being poor, unemployed and unemployable. To say nothing of having what her heart truly wants: satisfying work.*[15]

I remember a faculty discussion with my colleagues at Rollins College. Some enlightened leaders tried to get us to recognize the power differential between us and our students, especially between male faculty and female students. Our having authority over them increased the possibility that we could be successful in trying to take advantage of them, often sexual advantage, and also the possibility that they might succumb. As the discussion went on for an hour and a half, I realized that some of my male colleagues just did not get it. Systemic bias, systemic sexism.

WORK AND CHILDREN

From their twenties onward, women are often asked when they're going to get a boyfriend, get married, and/or have children, as if women's worth lies only in their marital status and in childbearing and rearing capabilities. In the twenty-first century this is what most people still believe: that a life without children is a life unfulfilled, that a woman who is unmarried and childless is an "Unwoman," to borrow Margaret Atwood's phrase.[16]

Marjorie Hall Davis met her first husband while they both studied at Cornell University, he in veterinary medicine and she in neurology. Marj earned a master's degree and could have easily continued on for her doctorate. But she followed her husband to Granby, Connecticut, where he became a partner in a veterinary clinic. After moving in and setting up their home, Marj took a position as a science teacher at the new Granby High School. She established the chemistry program and taught biology and chemistry.

Then, after three years teaching, she retired. She had to! Her contract read that if she got pregnant, she would have to retire at the end of the term

---

15. Angelson, "Good Girls Revolt Star" (italics mine). A power imbalance is a key ingredient of racism, of speciesism, of the Roman rule over Palestine at the time of Jesus, and of the colonization of much of the southern hemisphere by Europeans.

16. Robertson, "5 Examples of Everyday Sexism."

closest to the end of the first trimester of her pregnancy. If she came back after birthing her child, she would have to prove that he or she was cared for while she was teaching school. That was in the 1950s and no one talked about sexual discrimination. But systemic sexism it was.

There was a time in US history when women and men were treated more equally. During World War II, so many men went to war that there were not enough men available for the factory positions that made the weapons. So, women were hired into the industrial "war machine." Of course, when the war ended and the men came home, most of them returned to jobs in industry. And women returned home. However, many had worked and had found that work meaningful. So, many found employment, at lower than factory wages, in the developing service sector.

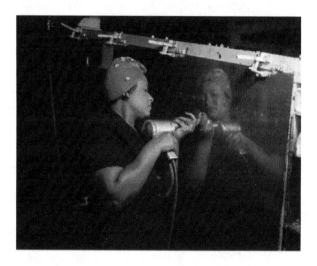

Fig. 23. Rosie the Riverter during World War II. This image is a work of an employee of the United States Farm Security Administration or Office of War Information domestic photographic units, taken as part of that person's official duties. As a work of the U.S. federal government, the image is in the public domain in the United States.

Ever since the agricultural revolution ten thousand years ago, the vast majority of the world's population has been engaged in farming. However, beginning in the nineteenth century, industrial employment took primacy over agricultural work in many countries. By the twenty-first century the service sector had come to represent the fastest-growing area of the workforce in the world's most advanced economies. In the United States, for example, the number of people engaged in service occupations in the 1950s already exceeded the number of workers thereafter.[17]

Furthermore, after the war a new kind of work developed. Women could run a sales franchise from their home, at times that suited them, while they raised the baby-boomer generation. Some became Avon Ladies and some held Tupperware Parties.

Fig. 24. The Avon Lady, https://diginomica.com/sites/default/files/stylesarticle_images_ desktop_2x/public/images/2018-02/AvonLady-e1518779523194.png?itok=_B96X09f.

Fig. 25. Tupperware Party. https://clickamericana.com/wp-content/uploads/Sixties-Tupperware-party-1963.jpg.

17. Kranzberg and Hannan, "History of the Organization of Work."

I remember my grandmother's Avon Lady. The three of us often went out for dinner. Back then I had no idea that sexism had been a "natural" part of societies for millennia—ever since the agricultural revolution with its cow and plow agriculture, ever since the Yamnaya replaced the existing European farmers, took the women, and spread their genes throughout Europe.

Systemic sexism has continued into the twenty-first century, and even until today. There have been decades, even centuries, of cultural mores that have restricted what women could do with their lives. Just fifty years ago single women met barriers in companies that prevented them from "rising" to more responsible positions. The barriers are often still there. Other mores made it difficult for women to join the workforce. Their job—unpaid—was to be homemakers, support their husbands, look nice at company gatherings, and raise children. I remember as I was growing up that, if a woman couldn't find a husband and had to work to support herself, she was called a "spinster."

Women could not get their own credit cards unless their husband signed for them. Highly intelligent women, high-school graduates, were not accepted at prestigious Ivy League universities. These and other mores prevented qualified women, who wanted more than homemaking, from flourishing. They were prevented from being unique human beings and contributing their own gifts to society. Such restriction limits a person's functioning well and in ways that support the larger social system. A system that does not help people function well is evil.

Fig 26. Spinster, https://www.google.com/search?q=spinster+cartoon+images+free &rlz.

SYSTEMIC RACISM. EVOLVED SKIN COLOR

As we migrated out of Africa into what later became Europe, an interesting thing happened to us. Our skin color changed—from dark brown to bronze to white. It was a matter of our survival because the intensity of sunlight changed as we moved north.[18]

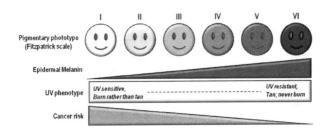

Fig. 27. Fitzpatrick Skin Color Scale, John D'Orazio, Stuart Jarrett, Alexandra Amaro-Ortiz and Timothy Scott—John D'Orazio et al. "UV Radiation and the Skin" Int. J. Mol. Sci. 2013, 14(6), 12222-12248; doi:10.3390/ijms140612222 http://www.mdpi.com/1422-0067/14/6/12222/htm, CC BY 3.0, File: Influence of pigmentation on skin cancer risk.png. Created: 7 June 2013.

Skin color is determined by the amount of melanin in our cells. Melanin is a pigment that acts as a sunscreen, so we don't get burned in the blazing equatorial sun. But when we Africans migrated to the north, we needed less of this sunscreen. With less we could capture more vitamin D from the sun. The variations occurred through Darwinian evolution. Random genetic variations related to skin color were selected by how well they helped us reproduce in a particular environment—the environment being sunlight. All this variation is natural. We are all siblings "under the skin."

From the systems perspective of this book, it is important that we think about doing evil as systemic. Even though one individual might do harm to another, much more harm can be done when a large and complex system is created that produces significant harm for many in the system. Let's return to reviewing some of our history.

You and I arrived in America from England in 1630. We were poor but still acquired farmland in Connecticut and built a life for ourselves. The new land was good for us. We even got along with the inhabitants who already

---

18 The Fitzpatrick skin-color scale on this page was developed in 1974 by dermatologist Thomas B. Fitzpatrick. It categorizes the response of different skin types to ultraviolet light, and it continues to be a recognized tool for research on human skin pigmentation.

lived there, the Wampanaug and other native tribes. However, we knew we were vastly outnumbered, so fear of these people with strange ways never left us. Our only real choice was to subdue them.

XENOPHOBIA—FEAR OF STRANGERS

We also feared the strangeness of many others who were not like us. In 1751, Benjamin Franklin expressed this deep fear with his worry about the Germans migrating to and settling Pennsylvania.

> Why should Pennsylvania, founded by the English, become a Colony of Aliens, who will shortly be so numerous as to Germanize us instead of our Anglifying them, and will never adopt our Language or Customs, any more than they can acquire our Complexion? . . . The Number of purely white People in the World is proportionably very small. All Africa is black or tawny. Asia chiefly tawny. America (exclusive of the new Comers) wholly so. And in Europe, the Spaniards, Italians, French, Russians and Swedes, are generally of what we call a swarthy complexion; as are the Germans also, the Saxons only excepted, who with the English, make the principal Body of White People on the Face of the Earth. I could wish their Numbers were increased.[19]

In the American colonies, white was the dominant skin color. Yet, we began to see a few dark-skinned people, some almost black, when we went to larger towns. They reminded you/me of us and our relatives while we were still in Africa thousands of years ago. We learned that they did not migrate to the New World voluntarily like we did. They were slaves, captured in their home countries and sold to slave traders—northern Europeans who packed them on crowded ships, below deck in filth and stench. Many died. Out of the 12.5 million Africans bought to our land between 1525 and 1866, 1.7 million perished on the transatlantic voyage.[20]

Over three and a half centuries I and you watched—and were part of—the creation of an unjust political-economic social system, created by government and by whites who were in power—systemic racism. At the

19. Yglesias, "Swarthy Germans."

20. Historians tell us that slavery can be found in all societies. There are two reasons for this. First, when someone becomes destitute, he or she enters into slavery under another person. Second, individuals or groups of people captured in war can become slaves of the conquerors. However, the capture of millions of dark-skinned Africans, transporting them across the Atlantic Ocean by people almost devoid of skin color, and selling them into slavery to white people occurs only once in human history.

core of the racist system was the growing of cotton in the South.[21] Most of the slaves went to plantations to help rich white people grow cotton, which made them even more wealthy. But not all slaves worked on cotton plantations. Many were slaves in well-to-do households throughout the colonies. Even here black people weren't treated well. You and I discovered that colonial and revolutionary leaders such as George Washington, Thomas Jefferson, James Madison, and Aaron Burr "sexually abused enslaved females working in their households" and produced biracial families.[22]

Moreover, free blacks continued to be discriminated against in many ways. (1) New medical surgeries and treatments were tried on blacks (usually women) before they were used on whites during the nineteenth and first half of the twentieth century.[23] (2) Black innovators were barred from filing patents for their inventions. (3) Poll taxes were levied on voters. Whites could afford the poll tax much more easily than blacks, thereby disenfranchising African American voters. (4) After the Civil War and the freeing of slaves, Jim Crow laws segregated blacks from whites: "It shall be unlawful for a negro and white person to play together or in company with each other in any game of cards or dice, dominoes or checkers" (Birmingham, Alabama, 1930). "Marriages are void when one party is a white person and the other is possessed of one-eighth or more negro, Japanese, or Chinese blood" (Nebraska, 1911). "Separate free schools shall be established for the education of children of African descent; and it shall be unlawful for any colored child to attend any white school, or any white child to attend a colored school" (Missouri, 1929). "All railroads carrying passengers in the state (other than street railroads) shall provide equal but separate accommodations for the white and colored races, by providing two or more passenger cars for each passenger train, or by dividing the cars by a partition, so as to secure separate accommodations" (Tennessee, 1891).

Even when blacks fought in the two world wars, they were marginalized. Jim Crow laws still applied in southern US bases. During the wars, blacks were relegated to service and support units because those in power did not think them fit for combat. Black nurses, many fewer than the number who wanted to serve, were assigned to nurse only black soldiers or German war prisoners.

When they returned home after World War II, blacks were shut out from many housing opportunities by "restrictive covenants." In communities

---

21. An earlier economic basis for the slavery of Africans was the growing of sugar in the Caribbean and South America.

22. Solly, "158 Resources," para. 10.

23. Holland, "Father of Modern Gynecology."

across the United States property owners signed agreements that barred African Americans (and sometimes other groups-including Jews, Asians, and Latinos) from their neighborhoods. For example, in a covenant from Arlington County, Virginia in the 1940s, purchasers agreed never to sell their house to "persons of any race other than the white Caucasian Race."

More extensive and hence more significant was the practice of redlining. "Redlining" came from the development by the "New Deal," that is by the federal government, of maps of every metropolitan area in the country. The maps were color coded by the Home Owners' Loan Corporation and then the Federal Housing Administration. The color codes were designed to indicate where it was safe to insure mortgages. Any area where black skinned people lived, or lived nearby, was colored red. You and I were told that this was to indicate to appraisers that these neighborhoods were too risky to insure mortgages. So, blacks could not get loans.[24]

Federal HOLC "Redlining" Map, Hartford area, 1937

Fig. 28. "Redlining" Hartford, CT, Mapping Inequality. Creative Commons License (CC BY-NC-SA 4.0).

In Hartford, Connecticut, the red zone is on the Connecticut River. You and I think this might be a nice area. But historically the river has been the main commercial link from northern New England to Long Island Sound and the Atlantic Ocean. So, industry grew in this part of Hartford, and the red area signified the least desirable and lowest priced property. To the left of the red zone on the map we see areas colored yellow, blue, and green. If we were to drive west from the river through these areas we would

24. *Encyclopaedia Britannica*, s.v. "Redlining," September 11, 2014, https://www.britannica.com/topic/redlining.

see that the color of most people's skin becomes lighter. And there are bigger houses, nearby stores, more green land. You and I realize that blacks and Hispanics will have a difficult time moving to better living conditions. The segregation, the racism is systemic. The system of the "land of the free and the home of the brave" is unjust. It is immoral.

SOME RESULTS OF SYSTEMIC OR STRUCTURAL RACISM

Asthma in Hartford, Connecticut

In a recent survey of rate of asthma in one hundred United States cities, Hartford, Connecticut, has the dubious distinction of being number 11. (Its neighbor to the north, Springfield, Massachusetts, is number 1.) Having an asthma attack feels like someone has put a pillow on your face and is holding it there. You can't breathe.

Hardest hit is the area of South Meadows, on the Connecticut River and adjacent to downtown Hartford (in the red zone). South Meadows is an area of run-down housing near an industrial area including three coal-fired power plants, and the home of small industry and rundown housing. When Blacks and Jamaicans migrated into Hartford, South Meadows was already in considerable decline. Its buildings were old and lacked repair. In apartments, carpets and furniture were full of mold, which was a significant cause of Asthma attacks. The most recent immigrants could only find and afford some of the poorest inner-city housing.

While city air pollution is one of the main causes, other pollutants also cause asthma, especially ozone and particulate matter. Hartford incinerates garbage for 66 Connecticut towns, as well as towns in New York, Massachusetts, and Vermont. Connecticut burns more of its garbage than any other state, and trash incineration produces air pollution and toxins that trigger asthma attacks. "Hartford is the dumping ground for the entire region," said Cynthia R. Jennings, chairwoman for Environmental Justice. "If it's dirty, it's in Hartford and we have to breathe it every day."[25]

Hartford is a good example of systemic racism. It's not only that individuals are racist, or even leaders of the community. I remember when the decision was made to dramatically increase incineration. In part, it was a solution to the existing landfill, near the Connecticut River. Some people in the area called the landfill "Mt. Hartford." And it was full! However, the new system was created without considering or ignoring the "unintended"

25. Tuhus, "High Rate of Asthma," section CN, p. 14.

consequences on people living in the area. The system was flawed. It was systemic evil.

Are things better twenty years later? Not really. In 2020 Hartford is ranked 4 of the one hundred asthma capitals of the country. (Springfield is 3, New Haven is 6, and Bridgeport is 8.)[26] It looks like systemic racism has increased, because these communities have a significant percentage of racial minorities. Individual racism is bad. Systemic racism is much worse. A dominant culture that discriminates against people is evil.

Lead Poisoning in Flint, Michigan

One of the great composers of all time was Ludwig von Beethoven, who died in 1827 at the age of fifty-six. New tests confirm that he suffered from lead poisoning. At the time Beethoven lived, possible sources of lead were wine sweetened with lead and wine goblets. Moreover, in his final weeks some of his treatment involved lead. Beethoven died in agony.

"Modern science shows that even low levels of lead can impair the brain development of fetuses, infants, and young children. The damage can reverberate for a lifetime, reducing IQ and physical growth and contributing to anemia, hearing impairment, cardiovascular disease, and behavioral problems. Large doses of lead exposure in adults have been linked to high blood pressure, heart and kidney disease, and reduced fertility."[27]

This happened in Flint, Michigan, a result of a flawed system and poor decisions by leaders. Some call what happened (or didn't happen) systemic racism. Flint was the original home of General Motors. However, since the 1980s the population dropped from 200,000 to 100,000. A majority are African Americans, and about 45 percent of Flint's residents live below the poverty line. Nearly one in six of the city's homes has been abandoned.

How did this happen? In an effort to save money the city leaders decided that Flint should end leasing fresh water from Detroit and use the Flint River instead. A dumping ground for industrial waste and for the city's sewage, the river produced horrible-tasting water. It began to cause skin rashes, hair loss, and itchy skin.

The Michigan Civil Rights Commission reviewed what was happening, listening to the testimony of many who were adversely affected. On February 17, 2017, it reported its findings: "Reviewing the historical governmental actions impacting the living and health conditions of Flint residents, i.e., the legacy of Flint, was sobering and left a deep impression.

26. AAFA, "2020 Allergy Capitals."

27. Denchak, "Flint Water Crisis."

We must come to terms with the ongoing effects of 'systemic racism' that repeatedly led to disparate racial outcomes as exemplified by the Flint Water Crisis. This can no longer be ignored."[28]

SYSTEMIC SPECIESISM: WHO HAS MORAL STANDING?

The beginning of Aldo Leopold's *Sand County Almanac* narrates a shocking story: "When God-like Odysseus returned from wars in Troy, he hanged all on one rope a dozen slave girls of his household whom he suspected of misbehavior during his absence. This hanging involved no question of propriety. The girls were property. The disposal of property was then, as is now, a matter of expediency, not of right and wrong."[29]

WHOSE FUTURE SHOULD YOU AND I BE CONCERNED ABOUT?

This is a very important, perhaps the most important ethical question. It is especially significant as we increasingly deal with climate change. Whose future should we be concerned about—only our own future, or also the future of our families and close friends, the future of our religious community, the future of our society, the future of the entire human community, the future of all sentient creatures, or the future of the entire planet earth and all that is part of earth? Questions regarding whose future you and I should be concerned about are questions about who is in the moral community.

Another way to explore this is to ask: "Who has moral standing?" For most of Western ethics, when people have thought about moral questions, it has been assumed that only humans have moral standing. And then, not even all humans. Those who are not fully capable of rational thought do not have moral standing; for the ancient Greeks this included women. Captured enemies did not have moral standing. Slaves did not have moral standing. People with skin of a different color did not have moral standing. Not having moral standing means that when those who have the power make decisions about what should be done, they do not have to consider the interests of these kinds of people—interests such as health, education, or the right to vote. People who lack moral standing are not full citizens of the community.

---

28. For a more general picture of the lead problem in other parts of the United States, see Ireland and Palmer, "Full Picture of Our Lead Problem."

29. Leopold, *Sand County Almanac*, 190.

In the last seventy-five years some ethicists have asked whether moral standing should be extended to women, animals, plants, and ecosystems. In what follows I will ask whether moral standing should be extended to everything on our planet and other parts of the universe on which we have an impact.

In light of my sketch about how You/I have come to be, it seems reasonable to say that everyone is family. We all—from atoms to neo-cortices—are interrelated. We might clarify this by imagining a sphere of concentric circles. This is a simplified version of what we spoke of earlier about everything being in dynamic relationships. At the center of the sphere is (1) a small circle that represents the physical earth prior to the emergence of life. (2) Around this is a second circle representing bacteria and other single-celled organisms. (3) Then a circle of plant species. (4) Next a circle of insects. (5) Then one of animals—sentient creatures. (6) Outside of this is the circle of humans as biological beings. (7) Next the circle of human social and political communities. (8) Then the circle of human culture including human technology. Finally, (9) the largest circle represents the earth as a whole, an extremely complex and dynamic, evolving relational system of all the circles and the interactions among them.

Thinking about all this we can ask again, who is in the moral community? Whose existence, well-being, and flourishing should be taken into account as we decide what we ought to do in the future that is ahead.

LOVE YOUR NEIGHBOR AS YOU LOVE YOURSELF

An earlier historical way of posing this question was to ask, "Who is our neighbor?" Or, in light of our story that implies we are related to everything else, are we all "family"? Should we love all things from atoms to humans as if we were family? Or, looking at the entire system and its 13.8 billion years of evolution, what are the implications regarding who has moral standing if everything that exists is a created co-creator?

CREATORS

Co-creators is another way of deciding who are members of the moral community. What I have called the cosmic moral family is from another point of view the creativity that gives rise to the history, the growth, and the overall flourishing of our cosmic family. Rooted in this understanding, I suggest that a second moral guideline is not only loving one's neighbor but also loving God—that is, loving not only created good but creative good. As we have seen, these two kinds of good are intertwined with one another in the ongoing evolution of the universe including earth, life on earth, human life, human culture, and human technology.

However, both creativity and what is created lead to what is morally bad if humans attempt to limit these two forms of good, to confine them only to preconceived visions about what the future should be like or who should be part the future. In this view, sin (the Christian term for human evil) is the attempt to limit the work of creativity (God) and to limit what is included in the family of life that arises from the work of creativity (God). Sin comes into play when we do not love the Lord our God (creativity) with all our heart and mind and soul and strength, and when we do not love our neighbors (the creatures of the created world) as ourselves. In other words, sin is based on not recognizing and admitting our limits as human, created co-creators. It is thinking that our solutions to particular, formulated problems are complete. It is thinking that nothing more needs to be taken into account. Sin is failing to recognize and take into account the limits of our visions. It is ignoring our finitude—even as created co-creators. Let me offer a few examples.

MORAL STANDING IN AN ERA OF CLIMATE CHANGE—SOME EXAMPLES

Not recognizing human finitude! Not recognizing the complexity of creativity and its variety of consequences—this is the sin of humans as created co-creators.

The Warming of the Oceans, the United States

Recognizing that everything is a created co-creator helps us look beyond our finitude, so that we can have greater awareness of carbon dioxide emissions and the resulting global warming. One of the most noticed effects of warming is the rise in sea levels because of melting glaciers adding water and of the expansion of sea water as it becomes warmer.

Sea level rise is noticeable along New England coasts as well as the more lasting danger of flooding in lower coastal regions around the world. A narrow vision of our role as created co-creators can lead to selfish responses, such as the hedge fund manager who bought, tore down a multimillion-dollar house right on the ocean, and then built a new multimillion-dollar house that is elevated. When the sea level rises and storms churn up the waves, they will flow *under* the house rather than flood it.

However, we might question whether this new home would have withstood the February 3, 2021, storm if it had received the direct hit that the eastern shore of Cape Cod and Massachusetts had. Like the November 7, 2012 Super Storm in the picture, the 2021 storm pummeled the Atlantic coast and left multiple collapsed and condemned homes. Heavy beach erosion along the coast of the state literally "took the ground" out from under them. A devastating combination of massive waves and a high tide sent coastal floodwaters slamming into the foundations of homes all along this coastal region. Multiple homes were completely toppled over and collapsed by the storm.

Fig. 29. 2012 Noreaster Superstorm

Today, August 31, 2021, is the birthday of my second-oldest grandchild.[30] In fifty years he will be my age. Last month was the birthday of my second-youngest grandchild. In sixty years she will be my age. What will they experience if they live on the eastern coastline of the United States and the yearly breaching of the "hundred-year flood plane."

When I began teaching in Florida in 1973, I became acquainted with some conservationists. One thing I learned was the idea of the "hundred-year flood plane." This was an area that one could expect to be flooded once every hundred years. Only a major weather event would cause such flooding. Imagine my shock when I read an article from *Nature Climate Change*,

---

30. My second marriage, to Marj Davis, in 1999, has given me seven grandchildren—ages nineteen to thirty-one. I wonder what our climate will be like when they reach my age, eighty-plus, in fifty or sixty years.

which was published a day before my grandson's birthday. It presented the results of some thorough scientific work. One conclusion was that with only a 1.5 foot increase in sea level, a number of areas (50% of more that 7,000 locations around the world) will experience hundred-year floods *every* year. Especially vulnerable areas are the eastern shore of the United States south of New York City.

The US coast that will be most affected by climate change, warming oceans, and flooding is Florida. In Miami sea level rise is already high enough so that at high tides and prevailing easterly winds, the streets of the city flood. As a response to this, Miami has raised millions of dollars to raise the streets. How long is this good for? About fifty years![31]

Fig. 30. Miami Beach in 2050. http://sealevel.climatecentral.org

Oceans Rising, Tuvalu. In June of 2015, Marj and I flew to California to participate in the exceptionally large conference on "Seizing an Alternative: Towards an Ecological Civilization," held at the colleges in Claremont, California. Every morning before the plenary session, an excellent fourteen-member folk band, The Pilgrim Pickers, from a nearby retirement center gave a concert, including some sing-along music. One of my favorites was composed and written by Jim Manly. It was called "Tuvalu." Tuvalu is a tiny group of islands between Hawaii and Australia. With a population of eleven thousand, it's the fourth smallest nation in the world. The highest point is only ten feet above sea level (think of a basketball hoop). A one-foot rise in sea level could make Tuvalu uninhabitable. Several times at the conference we sang this and similar songs.

31. Elvladyman, "Before the Flood."

Chorus:
Tuvalu Tuvalu
Tiny islands in the ocean blue,
Tuvalu Tuvalu
You live or die by what we do.

Verse 1:
Blue lagoon and coral sand
Mark the beauty of your land,
But the ice is melting far away
And the sea is rising in the bay.

Chorus

Verse 2:
Cyclones blowing to your grief
Coral dying on the reef
Fish no longer come in swarms
As the ocean water warms
Some still fight with tanks and guns
But a new war has begun
This is how the world attacks
With car exhaust and chimney stacks

Chorus

Verse 3:
Hear the island people say
Join us in more gentle ways,
Treat all life with precious worth
Live more simply on the earth
Atolls flood as rising seas
Swamp your homes and breadfruit trees
Time to leave, you cannot stay
Where to go, you cannot say.

Chorus[32]

In the examples we have just looked at the concern is about humans. Even those who discuss the future of Tuvalu usually consider what only effects humans. However, if we remember that everything in the universe is

---

32. Copyright 2007 by James K. Manley, all rights reserved, see www.manleymusic. com.

a part of our natural family, having been created over 13.8 billion years, sea level rise is not only making human living more and more difficult. It is also impacting microorganisms, plants, shellfish, and fish. Our development of the moral implications of billions of years of evolution also includes the welfare of all other forms of life.

The dramatic although limited responses to global warming reveal the trap of human short-sightedness. The underlying, extensive problems are not addressed, although many scientists and others are responding. These problems include the complete flooding of low elevation islands in the Pacific or of low lying settlements along the coast of Alaska; the bleaching of corals that leads to the death of countless sea creatures the corals shelter; sea life moving to new homelands in more northern, cooler oceans (lobsters are moving north from the coast of Maine, putting lobstermen out of work); more violent storms on sea and land as pressure gradients increase due to warming oceans; acidification of the oceans (carbon dioxide and water yields carbonic acid), which makes it more difficult for fish and other sea life to breathe; and perhaps most important the destruction of phytoplankton (one-celled plants) at the base of the ocean food chain. Phytoplankton "also gobble up carbon dioxide to produce half the world's oxygen output—equaling that of trees and plants on land."[33] Between 1950 and 2010 the phytoplankton population declined about 40 percent.[34]

Compared to these "ocean losses," building New England mansions under which storm waves can flow or raising streets so traffic can move another fifty years at Miami's high tides—such narrow-minded co-creating seems obscene. Being moral created co-creators is certainly a higher calling for humans than this.

So, what does it mean to be moral in the context of 13.8 billion years during which all things are created co-creators? What is the meaning of our own species as it has been created over thousands of years? When we consider the interests of all created co-creators on earth, we need to move beyond the obvious ways of problem solving that focus mostly on human interests. We need to become more aware in our specific circumstances of how we are part of processes much larger and older than we humans. We need to be aware of the complex earth systems that create and sustain us. And we need to orient ourselves to the greater good that is more than just human good. If God is the creativity of the universe and if we are self-aware, imaginative co-creators, then the scope of our intentional participation in creativity must be much more expansive than thinking about what is good for humans alone.

33. Morello, "Phytoplankton Population."
34. Boyce et al., "Global Phytoplankton Decline," 591–96.

In the next two chapters about Jesus—what he did and who he was—and in the following two chapters on practicing Christianity, we will explore some ways that "naturalistic Christians" who follow the way of Jesus can respond right now to human evil—to sexism, racism, and speciesism.

5

SALVATION: WHAT DID JESUS DO?

IN THIS CHAPTER I will look at two different Christian understandings of salvation. One understands salvation as "rescue." Rescue from what? From God's negative judgment, because all people have sinned and broken their relationship with God. And those who have broken their relationship with God will be punished. This means everyone. Notice that this view is consistent with the worldview of biblical times or of the time of Dante.

The second understanding fits a dynamic, systems understanding of parts that are or are not well-integrated in a larger whole. When parts are not integrated within an individual or a community, when they work at odds with each other, the system does not function well. It is diseased or broken. When parts of a person or community are functioning well together, the system is whole and healthy. Moving from being a broken system to one that is a well-functioning whole is salvation. It's called "salvation" because the word *salvus* in Latin means "to heal."

In the first chapter of this book we journeyed two thousand years from the time of the biblical worldview to the medieval worldview and then to the worldview of contemporary science. In chapter 3 I developed the contemporary scientific story of the universe from the grammatical perspective of first-person singular, so that the history of the universe is my own personal story and, if you take my point of view, your story as well.

In this chapter I will use another approach—namely, how through my own experience growing up I came to understand what salvation can mean for a Christian in light of contemporary science.

When I was growing up in Christianity, my idea of salvation assumed a combination of the worldviews of biblical times and the Middle Ages. I call it a dualistic understanding of salvation. I am saved from sin, converted to being a follower of Jesus, and have eternal life. This dualism of sin and salvation also includes the historical Middle Age's prospect of hell and the expectation of heaven.

Today, in terms of systems thinking, we can think in terms of competing parts, and of some parts dominating other parts or subsystems. In a family, a parent may dominate to the point of abusing the children. On school grounds, a bully may upset cooperative activity. People elected to public office may exert their influence to shape governing a city or a nation for their own benefit. Or one nation may engage in war with another and, after winning, annex the defeated country as second-class people. Racism is also an example of one part of society dominating another.

On the other hand, salvation is freeing the dominated or oppressed, and recreating a well-functioning whole. I call this the "health model" of salvation. The goal is the facilitating all parts of the system to interact in dynamic harmony. Some point out that the usual metaphor or image for Darwinian evolution is "survival of the fittest." However, cell biologist Ursula Goodenough says the appropriate metaphor or image is really "survival of those who fit in"—well-functioning parts that contribute to the well-functioning of a larger system.

Interestingly, I think that this understanding can also be seen in the vices and virtues of Dante's *Divine Comedy*: the spheres of hell are for those who exhibit lust, gluttony, greed, anger, heresy, violence, fraud, treachery. How could a society of people like this continue and flourish? The vices lead to broken systems. So do the similar vices that are to be overcome in purgatory. Interestingly they all involve love—but it is perverted love. The three categories of perverted love are (1) the excessive love of lust, gluttony, and greed, (2) the deficient love of sloth, and (3) the malicious love of wrath, envy, and pride. Again, how could a system of humans such as a family, church, or nation survive with people caught under control of such vices? The difference between hell and purgatory is that in purgatory the vices can be overcome. In hell there is no hope. Imagine a human community—how about a local church—in which people's vices destroy the community. The only viable way forward is the destruction of the old community and replacement by another healthy community.

A healed or whole system is portrayed by the virtues that are the final way-stations for Dante, as he is led by Beatrice to make his way to God. His life begins to function well with the four cardinal virtues—temperance, fortitude, justice, and prudence—and the three theological virtues—faith, hope, and charity or self-giving love. Can we imagine a human community with people possessing these virtues? Wouldn't it be a dynamic system that functions well as it fits into other larger systems, and finally into the entire complex system of planet earth?

EXODUS COMES BEFORE GENESIS

Now I'll pick up again on my own story, in order to develop the two primary understandings of what Jesus did and who Jesus was—the two understandings of the atonement I've just stated. What Jesus did is the focus of the rest of this chapter. What Jesus was is brought to light in chapter 6.

When I was twenty-one, I entered McCormick Seminary in Chicago to study to become a minister. One of my first classes was Old Testament, (now usually called Hebrew Bible). The professor George Knight spoke with a delightful Scottish accent—quite appropriate for a scholar. Class session after class session he would amaze us with his surprising insights about the Bible. None was more surprising than when, at the beginning of one lecture he proclaimed, "Exodus comes before Genesis." What?!

As I followed his thinking, I came to understand that Knight did not mean "before" in time, in history. Rather, with his phrase "Exodus before Genesis" he was pointing that the first experience the ancient Hebrews had of God was their liberation from slavery in Egypt and the establishment of their community under the laws of Yahweh. The ten commandments in Exodus 20 refer to this liberation: "And God spoke all these words: 'I am the Lord your God, who brought you out of Egypt, out of the land of slavery'" (Exod 20:1–3). Here is the core of the Jewish and Christian understanding of God—God is on the side of the enslaved or oppressed.

The commandments that follow are related to the emerging community as a "well-functioning system." The theme is that whatever breaks up the newly formed system is forbidden. The first four commandments establish that the community (system) has its center in the creator of the community; in terms of my second chapter the center is creativity: (1) You shall have no other Gods but me. (2) You shall not make for yourself any idol, nor bow down to it or worship it. (3) You shall not misuse the name of the Lord your God. (4) You shall remember and keep the Sabbath day holy.

Two of the next commandments preserve the family unit. (5) Respect your father and mother, (7) You must not commit adultery.

The final four apply to the wider society. (6) You must not commit murder. (8) You must not steal. (9) You must not give false evidence against your neighbor. (10) You must not be envious of your neighbor's goods. You shall not be envious of his house or his wife, or anything that belongs to your neighbor.

From a contemporary evolutionary perspective, these commandments look like they set the boundaries that will help a group survive and flourish. The overall result looks like a dynamic well-functioning system.

MY STORY GROWING UP IN CHRISTIANITY, LEAVING IT, AND FINALLY RETURNING

The Presbyterian church I grew up in, from kindergarten through high school graduation, was a liberal church. My parents were liberal in their Christian faith. They practiced their Christianity by serving others.

When I was in seventh grade, I went to Camp Onaway. Onaway was a Presbyterian church camp on an island in a chain of lakes near Waupaca, Wisconsin. There I grew in my own faith over four years of weeklong youth conferences until I entered my sophomore year in high school. Then, at that conference, I had an experience that established the general course of my life. My father was a mechanical engineer, designing and overseeing the manufacture of milk processing and cheese making equipment in the "dairy state." During my junior high years (seventh through ninth grades), I thought I too would become an engineer. However, my minister (he and his wife were like uncle and aunt) told me I would make a fine minister. That had some appeal to me, because more than anything else I wanted a career and a life in which I could help people. So, a strange conflict emerged, an unlikely set of career choices—minister or engineer.

This conflict set the stage for a "conversion" experience at Camp Onaway. That summer I did not even plan to go to the camp, but my minister got me a scholarship. I couldn't refuse. When I got to camp, much to my surprise, I was elected president. (I also found my first girlfriend.) One task of the president was to be one of the leaders of the Friday night consecration service. It was held in a beautiful outdoor chapel in the midst of pine trees on a hill overlooking the lake. Before the service every camper filled out a form reconfirming his or her faith in Jesus Christ. Also, on the form was a place where you could state your intended career, including your interest in a Christian vocation. I wrote that I wanted to be an engineer.

However, when my time came to read the scripture, I looked out at the congregation of my fellow campers and our counselors. Suddenly, I realized—and said to myself—"this is where I belong!" *This is where I belong.* Since that moment I have never wavered in my commitment. What that commitment was became clear the next morning when I met with a small group of campers and some of the ministers. When asked why I wanted to enter the ministry, I responded, "I want to help people." I had decided that the ministry was a profession devoted primarily to helping people. Ministering to people meant helping them.

The ministers stared at me, "Well . . . ?" I sensed that I should say more. But why wasn't a commitment to helping people enough? I forgot what I said, but it did not diverge from my idea of helping. Finally, I was accepted as a youth who would go under "care of the Presbytery." A Presbytery is composed of ministers and lay leaders from several churches in a given region. My region, "Winnebago Presbytery," included thirty-one churches in the northeastern third of the state of Wisconsin.

My camp experience, resulting in my turning toward a career in ministry, had significant ramifications for my future. The most important was where I would go to college. If I had followed my father, it would have been the engineering school at the University of Wisconsin in Madison. If I went into ministry, it made sense to go to a Presbyterian church college, Carroll College in Waukesha, Wisconsin, just west of Milwaukee.

In September 1957 I began my four years at Carroll. In the spring of my first year I became a close friend with two sophomores, Chuck and Clint. One of the things that bothered me about the college was that it called itself a "Christian College," but other than a once-a-week chapel service, which all freshman had to attend, I didn't see much evidence of Christianity. That was not the case with Chuck and Clint; they were really devout Christians, praying together at the beginning of each day, studying the Bible, and witnessing to others about Jesus. They also were members of an international organization called the "Navigators."

The Navigators is an international, interdenominational Christian ministry established in 1933. Their motto is: "To know Christ, make Him known, and help others do the same." This is done through building "Life-to-Life" mentoring—or discipling—relationships among Christ followers, equipping them to make an impact on the people around them for God's glory.[1]

I liked the sound of this. Here was a way to be Christian at Carroll College. So, I joined Chuck and Clint. We had a regular, rigorous discipline: pray for an hour at 5 a.m. each morning in the second-floor lounge of the Student Union. At 6 a.m. engage for an hour of Bible study. At 7 go to breakfast in the Student Union cafeteria. Then each of us went to classes. During the day we were expected to witness one-on-one to our fellow students, so they "would be saved" and commit to Christ. I witnessed to every girl I dated: "Have you committed your life to Christ as Lord and Savior?" At

---

1. See the Navigators website, https://www.navigators.org/about/.

the end of the day or weekend, we reported back to each other about what we did and whether we thought we were successful in witnessing. In the evening we did class preparation, and sometimes more Bible study.

During each day we took our packet of "Bible verse cards" and memorized them. These were single verse 2 x 3–inch cards that had been selected and organized into topical categories by people at national Navigator headquarters. The assumption was that each verse stood on its own. Here is the second of five major categories:

Proclaiming Christ

All Have Sinned	Romans 3:23	Isaiah 53:6
Sin's Penalty	Romans 6:23	Hebrews 9:27
Christ Paid the Penalty	Romans 5:8	1 Peter 3:18
Salvation is not by Works	Ephesians 2:8, 9	Titus 3:5
Must Receive Christ	John 1:12	Revelation 3:20
Assurance of Salvation	1 John 5:13	John 5:24

These topics and verses illustrate one of the two major understandings of salvation, the substitutionary atonement theory (the other is the moral exemplar theory). They also illustrate a particular understanding of the Bible. The Bible is the word of God and this means that individual verses of the Bible—each one of them—is a possible guide Christian living. (That individual verses might contradict one another does not seem to be considered.)

A second understanding of the Bible has been developed by biblical scholars during the nineteenth and twentieth centuries, the historical-critical approach. This is similar to what is used in studying other literary texts, such as the writings of Shakespeare. It focuses on stories and major themes in the history of Israel and early Christianity, and it sets the stories in particular historical contexts. Individual verses are part of what a wider text is saying.

MCCORMICK SEMINARY

When I attended McCormick Seminary, I learned that my experiences of (1) growing up in a liberal Christian family and church and (2) becoming a Navigator at Carroll College actually reflected the two primary theological theories of Christian atonement. "Atonement" is derived from the English vocabulary. An easy way to understand its meaning is "at-one-ment," how do God and humans become united? In particular, what did Jesus do that accomplished the uniting or reuniting?

One Christian theory is based on the example of sacrifice and focuses on interpreting the meaning of the crucifixion. The other theory focuses on the life and teachings of Jesus and of acquiring a "Christlike" mind, and of following Christlike love.

So: What did Jesus do for us? I'd like to develop the two quite different understandings I've already sketched. I'd also like to relate these understandings to the worldviews outlined in chapter 1.

WHAT DID JESUS DO?

In seminary I learned that the one of the most important Christian questions was the meaning of Jesus's death on the cross, the crucifixion. In the New Testament there is considerable uniformity among the four gospels about occurrences surrounding Jesus's death—especially when compared to the resurrection accounts of which there is almost no similarity. Because of its centrality in the climax of Jesus's life, I can't help but wonder why it was so important and what is its meaning? Over the centuries there have been several understandings of why Jesus died the horrible death of crucifixion. Theologian Ted Peters describes six. I'll simply name them and then focus on 2 and 4. (1) Jesus as the Teacher of True Knowledge; (2) Jesus as Moral Example and Influence; (3) Jesus as Victorious Champion; (4) Jesus as Satisfaction; (5) Jesus as the Happy Exchange; (6) Jesus as the Final Scapegoat.[2]

These are about *what Jesus did* and *who Jesus was.* The basic idea of each is that Jesus brought humans who were estranged from God back into relationship with God.

THE SUBSTITUTIONARY THEORY OF ATONEMENT

The core idea of this theory is that Jesus's death was a sacrifice for our sins, which led to God's forgiveness and reestablished our relationship with God.

Reestablishment of our relationship by sacrifice is found throughout the Bible. Its roots go back to the time of Moses. Moses was the "lawgiver" of Israel, but his brother Aaron and all Aaron's descendants were the priests. They were even the priests of the Jerusalem temple at the time of Jesus. The first seven chapters of the biblical book of Leviticus describes the procedures for seven different kinds of sacrifices of cattle, goats, sheep, turtle doves,

2. Peters, "Models of Atonement."

pigeons, and grain. These were brought to the priests to be offered to God. Why? To atone for the sins of the person who brought the sacrifice. What sins? Breaking any of the ten commandments and a multitude of other laws. Devout Jews calculate that there are 613 commandments they should follow.

Sacrifice of an animal or grain may seem strange, but it makes sense. Think of it as a meal to repair or heal a broken relationship. Suppose you have done something that angers a good friend, and she or he breaks off the relationship. You want to get your friend back. So, you invite her/him to dinner as a way of making amends. This is the idea behind the sacrifices in the Hebrew Bible. The burning of animals and offering of grains is creating a meal for God. How does God partake of the meal? God breathes in the smoke; that's the connection. If God is a spiritual being, this makes some sense—smoke rising up to the ultimate divine spirit, arising from the altar on which an animal is burning as a sacrifice. This is pleasing to God and the broken relationship is reestablished.

Interestingly, not all broken relations with God require sacrifices. (This is important.) A significant example is the story of Moses receiving the ten commandments. It took forty days. People at the base of Mt. Sinai got restless, and they created a golden calf to worship. When Moses came down from the mountain and saw this, he was so angry that he smashed the stone tablets on which the commandments were written. But then, relenting, Moses returned to the mountain to find that God also was angry. Here's what ensued, beginning with Exod 32:7:

> The Lord said to Moses, "Go down at once! Your people, whom you brought up out of the land of Egypt, have acted perversely; they have been quick to turn aside from the way that I commanded them; they have cast for themselves an image of a calf, and have worshiped it and sacrificed to it, and said, 'These are your gods, O Israel, who brought you up out of the land of Egypt!'" The Lord said to Moses, "I have seen this people, how stiff-necked they are. Now let me alone, so that my wrath may burn hot against them and I may consume them; and of you I will make a great nation." But Moses implored the Lord his God, and said, "O Lord, why does your wrath burn hot against your people, whom you brought out of the land of Egypt with great power and with a mighty hand? Why should the Egyptians say, 'It was with evil intent that he brought them out to kill them in the mountains, and to consume them from the face of the earth'? Turn from your fierce wrath; change your mind and do not bring disaster on your people. Remember Abraham, Isaac, and Israel, your servants, how you swore to them by your own

self, saying to them, 'I will multiply your descendants like the stars of heaven, and all this land that I have promised I will give to your descendants, and they shall inherit it forever.'" And the Lord changed his mind about the disaster that he planned to bring on his people. (Exod 32:7–14)

The idea of sacrifice, often with blood, carries over into Christianity as one of the ways of understanding the meaning of the crucifixion of Jesus. Jesus is symbolized as the lamb that is sacrificed. Jesus's blood is life giving. In the ancient Jewish sacrifices, blood is the life of an animal; life is in the blood of any animal including human beings. So, as gory as it may appear, the shedding of blood is salvific. So are grain offerings, because grain sustains life.

The idea of the sacrifice of Jesus on the cross was present since the origin of Christianity in both idea and ritual. Christ suffered and died for the "sins of the world." And this is enacted in the service of Holy Communion: the bread and wine *become* (Catholic) or *represent* (Protestant) the body of blood of Christ.

But how did Jesus Christ's dying on the cross actually accomplish atonement? What was the "mechanism" by which sins were forgiven? Why couldn't they be forgiven without Jesus's crucifixion?

The most interesting theological theory of how Jesus accomplished the forgiveness of sins was developed by Anselm of Canterbury (1033/34–1109.) He published what is called the "Satisfaction Theory" in 1099.[3] What needs to be satisfied is God's justice. The theory is actually a logical argument about "Why God Became Human"—*Cur Deus Homo*. Here's my paraphrase. The theory begins with (1) an assumption that all humans are created by God; for this they owe God complete obedience—100 percent obedience. (2) Each human being fails in giving God complete obedience. (3) God is a God of justice.[4] (4) Therefore, disobedience must be compensated for. If each of us owes God 100 percent obedience and we fail in this, we now owe God our Creator more that 100 percent, say 110 percent. (5) But how can we pay back more that 100 percent. We can't. Therefore, we must receive God's punishment and, as Paul says, the wages of sin is death, not eternal bliss after death with God (Romans 6). (6) Some might add that the punishment is eternity in hell. (Anselm did not go this far in his argument; do you think that perhaps Dante's *Divine Comedy* went this far?)

3. Kerr, *Readings in Christian Thought*, 85–93.

4. The meaning of the word *justice* in Anselm's argument is retribution—retributive justice. Receiving one's just deserts. Another important meaning is "distributive justice"—distributing what is good fairly to everyone. This understanding is more in keeping with the second theory of atonement, represented by Abelard.

So, how can we be saved? (7) Jesus died for our sins. (8) But how could Jesus's death satisfy God's justice. How could the death of single human being be a sacrifice for all people? (9) The answer is that Jesus was not just a human being. He was the Son of God. Earlier in Christian history the leaders of the church at the Counsel of Chalcedon (451 CE), decided that Jesus was fully man *and* fully God, completely human *and* completely divine. He was the God-Man.

So, *what did Jesus do?* Anselm built his argument on this idea of the God-man and said: only a human can die to satisfy God's justice and be forgiven. However, only God can pay the debt, can give more than 100 percent to pay humanity's great debt. There is only one who can satisfy both requirements—Jesus Christ who is completely human and completely divine. His sacrifice on the Cross, therefore, brings salvation to humanity.

One more thing must happen for a person to be saved. Jesus's death on the cross was an objective form of atonement—atonement outside of you and me. To work for us, atonement must become subjective—something in us. We must accept what Jesus did in faith that this is the way to salvation, to being reunited with God.

A part of accepting Jesus is to participate in the seven sacraments, especially confession and Holy Communion. In Holy Communion a communal meal takes place between human beings and God. Jesus is the Holy meal that does this—the sacrifice. By blessing the bread and the wine, these elements are transformed in reality (the Roman Catholic view) or in memory (a Protestant view) so that eating and drinking these elements becomes consuming the crucified, sacrificed Christ. This unites the worshippers with God.

I admire Anselm's use of logic. However, two questions can be asked: (1) what kind of God does Anselm present to us? And (2) how far back does the substitutionary theory of atonement go in Christian history?

Anselm's understanding of God is clearly that of a personal being, an absolute monarch, a king to which humans owe complete obedience. It fits nicely with the worldviews of two thousand and one thousand years ago, the worldviews from biblical times up to the rise of Western democracy. But how does it fit with today's understanding? What if you grew up in a family with a father who was an absolute authority, and it was fair if he punished you severely for any instance of disobedience? Led by feminist theologians, many today would say that this kind of God is a "child abuser." What kind of God would condone the suffering of his son by an extremely cruel and tortuous death, in order to forgive the wrongdoing of others? What kind of example does this bring to those who follow God?

The second question is how far back does the substitutionary theory go in Christian history? Of course, as we have seen, the idea of sacrifice is as old as ancient Israel. And the idea of sacrifice is in the New Testament, especially in the book of Hebrews. But how prominent was it as Christianity grew through the centuries.

Today we are a reading culture, and words-words-words are all over the place. The fact that we learn to read opens up new worlds of imagination. However, for many centuries the rate of literacy was quite low, perhaps 6 percent to 20 percent as we said in chapter 1. Even most of the priests were illiterate. So how did people learn about Christ and salvation?

Of course, one could learn about things, including religious matters, by word of mouth. But a more public way of communicating was visual— sculptures, paintings, mosaics, and stained-glass windows.

In their book *Saving Paradise*, theologians Rita Nakashima Brock and Rebecca Ann Parker ask how the message of Jesus was presented to Christians in the first centuries. To answer it, they explore Christian art. Looking at art is one way that people learn about events. So, what did people learn about Jesus? It was not about crucifixion and suffering. What was represented extensively in art for the early Christians was paradise—paradise on earth.

Brock and Parker write that as they visited ancient sites, consulted with art historians, and read ancient texts, they were "astonished at the weight of the reality: Jesus's dead body was just not there." Not in the catacombs or Rome's early churches. Not in Ravenna's mosaics. And not in Hagia Sophia, the great cathedral from the sixth century in Istanbul, or in the monastery churches in northeastern Turkey.

So, they began to look for what was depicted. Surprisingly, it was paradise. This was the dominant image of early Christianity. And paradise was not about "heaven" or the afterlife. It was on earth, this world permeated by the Spirit of God. "Images in Rome and Ravenna captured the craggy, scruffy pastoral landscape, the orchards, the clear night skies, and teeming waters of the Mediterranean world, as if they were lit by a power from within. Sparkling mosaics in vivid colors captured the world's luminosity. The images filled the walls of spaces in which liturgies fostered aesthetic, emotional, spiritual, and intellectual experiences of life in the present, in a world created as good and delightful."[5]

5. Brock and Parker, *Saving Paradise*, xv.

Fig. 31. St. Apollinarie in Classe, Ravenna, Italy Photo by Roger Culos Culos. CC BY-SA 3.0. Created October 5, 2015.

This all changed in the ninth century when Charlemagne conquered the Saxons in northern Germany and surrounding territories after thirty years of brutal warfare (772–804). The struggle was "marked by pillaging, broken truces, hostage taking, mass killings, deportation of rebellious Saxons, draconian measures to compel acceptance of Christianity, and occasional Frankish defeats."[6] Part of Charlemagne's strategy was to require that every conquered person be baptized or be put to death. With this he not only conquered land; he destroyed the Saxon culture with its older Germanic ideas and rituals.

Fig. 32. Crucifix in Cologne Cathedral

6. Sullivan, "Charlemagne," para. 8.

When this happened, as Brock and Parker observe, painters and sculpturers began to portray the suffering of their people—a subjugated people—with the suffering of Christ. The earliest crucifixes that depicted the agony and suffering of Jesus became a part of the religion of the conquered Saxons. The most prominent extant early crucifix is in the cathedral in Cologne, Germany. Today crucifixes are present in households too numerous to count, even mine. However, Brock and Parker argue that today we must regain paradise in opposition to religions supporting empires that are unjust and bring about much suffering.

THE MORAL INFLUENCE THEORY OF ATONEMENT

As part of regaining paradise on earth, we can examine another theory of atonement. Not too long after Anselm's satisfaction theory, in opposition to Anselm, another theory was advocated—the moral influence theory of Peter Abelard (1079–1142 CE).[7] This theory holds that Jesus reveals the heart of God by his example of love, selfless and unconditional love for others. A love that will even accept a cruel death. Such love inspires us to live our lives in the same way, with the same kind of love and the willingness to lay down our lives for others. Ted Peters says that the symbol for this kind of unconditional self-giving for others is the pelican. Imagine a family of starving pelicans. No food is available. The mother pelican is dedicated to the survival of her chicks. Rather than see them starve, she pecks at her own chest until a wound opens up. Then she plucks meat from her own heart to feed her young. This results in her death. But her children live. In European Christianity, the pelican-in-her-piety is often a symbol of God's love revealed in Jesus Christ.[8]

---

7. Kerr, *Readings in Christian Thought*, 93–95.

8. Peters, "Models of Atonement."

Fig 33. Pelican Sacrificing Herself to Feed Her Offspring
Montrealais, CC BY-SA 3.0, via Wikimedia Commons

There is more to what Jesus did than provide an example. In the theology of Peter Abelard (1079–1142), the story of God's love for us is inspiring. It is so inspiring that to hear the gospel of God's love transforms us. It has the power to turn our hearts toward caring for others. "Love answers loves' appeal." The result of this influence is that we can actually love self-sacrificially. When we love self-sacrificially, we are participating in the very love of God and establishing God's kingdom on earth. This is salvation.

Our response to Jesus can take the form of the following hymn by Congregational minister Washington Gladen.

> 1 O Master, let me walk with Thee
> in lowly paths of service free;
> tell me Thy secret; help me bear
> the strain of toil, the fret of care.

> 2 Help me the slow of heart to move
> by some clear, winning word of love;
> teach me the wayward feet to stay,
> and guide them in the homeward way.

> 3 Teach me Thy patience, still with Thee
> in closer, dearer company,
> in work that keeps faith sweet and strong,
> in trust that triumphs over wrong.

4 In hope that sends a shining ray
far down the future's broad'ning way;
in peace that only Thou canst give,
with Thee, O let me live.[9]

To walk with Jesus as love, to live like Jesus in love, to do what Jesus would do as a result of Christ-like love. This is the way to help bring paradise on earth.

---

9. Gladden, "O Master."

6

WHO/WHAT WAS JESUS?

WHAT UNDERSTANDING OF JESUS IS COMPATIBLE WITH THE MORAL EXAMPLE/INSPIRATION UNDERSTANDING OF ATONEMENT?

To begin to answer this, we must look at when and where Jesus lived and grew up. Traditions based on the Gospels of Matthew and Luke say that Jesus was born in Bethlehem. Some historians think this is not actual but is a way to link Jesus to David. Bethlehem is the "city of David." However, it is not disputed that Jesus grew up in Nazareth, a poor village of about four hundred inhabitants. Many were farmers; some were in other professions. Joseph was a carpenter or probably a stone mason or construction worker. When Jesus was old enough, he became an apprentice to his father. So, he too was probably a construction worker.

There was some work in Nazareth but there was a lot more work only four miles away in Sepphoris. At the time of Jesus, Sepphoris was the second-largest city in Palestine. Jerusalem was the first. Sepphoris was occupied by the Romans, but it also had a large population of wealthy Jews.

For the well-off Jews, Roman occupation was acceptable. However, lower-class Jews were not always happy and sometimes rebelled. After Herod the Great, who ruled all of Palestine, died in 6 BCE, the country was divided into five districts. One was Galilee, whose ruler was Herod Antipas, a son of Herod the Great. About the time Jesus was born in 4 BCE, a rebellion occurred, led by Judas the Galilean. Judas and his small army of zealots made a daring assault on the city of Sepphoris. They broke open the city's royal armory and seized for themselves the weapons and provisions that were stored inside. Now fully armed and joined by a number of sympathetic Sepphoreans, Judas and his followers launched a guerrilla war throughout Galilee, plundering the homes of the wealthy and powerful, setting villages ablaze, and meting out the justice of God upon the Jewish aristocracy and those who continued to pledge their loyalty to Rome. This continued for about ten years, until Judas and his followers mounted an all-out rebellion against the census/taxation of Quirinius. Judas thought that God was the sole "owner" of the land, so that taxation was a direct affront against God.

"Not long after he led the charge against the census, Judas the Galilean was captured by Rome and killed. As retribution for the city's having given up its arms to Judas's followers, the Romans marched to Sepphoris and burned it to the ground. The men were slaughtered, the women and children auctioned off as slaves. More than two thousand rebels and sympathizers were crucified en masse."[1]

JESUS'S BIRTH

How can we understand Jesus's birth within our naturalistic framework (no supernatural God) and in light of the events we have just described? How can we understand the situation of Mary, then little more than a girl when she was betrothed to an older man, Joseph? How did Mary become pregnant? Could Joseph be the one, he and Mary having had sex while engaged? Or, could Mary have been in a relationship with another man? New Testament scholar James Tabor thinks that Mary got pregnant as a result of a consenting relationship with the Roman soldier Pantera.[2] Whether Joseph or Pantera, the birth of Jesus would be compatible with our naturalistic worldview.

The most intriguing explanation from our naturalistic perspective—which considers the tumultuous times during which she lived—was that Mary was raped by Pantera.[3]

There are a number of reasons supporting the rape hypothesis. The first two reasons also support a consenting relationship between Mary and Pantera.

1. Aslan, *Zealot*, 43.

2. Tabor, "'Historical Look at the Birth of Jesus."

3. For dramatic and controversial videos about this, see Calisto Monserratt, "Mary Mother of Jesus."

First, by the end of the first century, there were rumors in some Jewish circles that Jesus was illegitimate. There is an interesting passage in the Gospel of John (John 8:41), written about seventy years after the birth of Jesus. In an argument that Jesus is having with some Jews, they say to Jesus: "We are not illegitimate children; we have one Father, God himself." Are they suggesting that Jesus is illegitimate? And why would John even include such an idea?

Second, in the last quarter of the second century, the anti-Christian Greek philosopher Celsius (ca. 177) wrote that some Jews had said Jesus's father was a Roman soldier named Pantera. (This comes from Origin's rebuttal of Celsius.)

Third, it was not unknown that the births of great men (they were all men) involved their being "sons of God." The miraculous births in these stories show their audiences that these god-men were different from regular men. Alexander the Great was said to be the result of his mother being impregnated by one of Zeus' thunderbolts. Several Greek demigods were said to have been the result of a conception between Zeus and a woman—Hercules, Dionysus, and Perseus most notably. The famous Greek philosopher Plato was said to be born of a virgin and the god Apollo. Romulus, the founder and first king of Rome, was said to be birthed from a virgin conceived with the god Mars. The first Roman emperor Augustus was the son of the God Apollo, conceived by a holy snake. Augustus ruled from 62 BCE to 14 CE. As you can see, in the first-century mind, Jesus was just one of many men said to be of divine origin by a miraculous birth.[4]

Fourth, if we consider when Matthew and Luke were written, it can be suggested that their birth narratives, seeming to narrate a "virgin birth," were composed to counter Roman claims about how Jesus came to be born. In doing so, Matthew and Luke were claiming that the conception and birth of Jesus, their Lord, was equivalent to the conception and birth of the emperor of Rome. "When Caesar Augustus (62 BCE–14 CE) was claimed to have been the son of Apollo, it wasn't to show *how Apollo had done a miracle*, it was to show that Augustus was a son of god and had a right to rule. The Gospel writers seem to have had a very specific reason for the miraculous virgin birth of Jesus: there was a new king in town."[5]

Furthermore, if one examines the birth narratives in Matthew and Luke, one finds some interesting ideas implied about Mary. In Matthew's opening genealogy, four women are in the list of ancestors of Jesus. This itself is very unusual. They are Tamar, who accepted being mistakenly treated

4. See *Rival Nations*, "One of Many Virgin Births."
5. *Rival Nations*, "One of Many Virgin Births."

as a prostitute and used it to her advantage (Genesis 38); Rahab, who is a prostitute in Jericho welcoming and consorting with her enemies, who were sent by Joshua (Joshua 2); Ruth sleeping with Boaz before marriage (Ruth 1–4); and Bathsheba, the wife of Uriah, committing adultery with David (2 Samuel 11–12). The fifth woman is Mary the mother Jesus. What point is Matthew trying to make? Why is Mary presented as a descendant of these four women? Is she also involved in sexual relations before marriage, whether with or without her approval? The activities of Mary's women ancestors seem to fit better with her being raped or having illicit sex than with her being a "pure" virgin.

In reading Luke's Gospel the same conclusion seems possible. Let's look at Mary's moving song of praise, the Magnificat. It begins with Mary speaking of the favor God has bestowed on his lowly servant. Then in v. 50 there is a sudden shift to Mary speaking about a mighty God of justice. I ask some questions of my own to suggest the possibility of Roman domination and Mary's rape.

Mary said,

> My soul magnifies the Lord,
> and my spirit rejoices in God my Savior,
>> *Why is God her Savior?*
> for he has looked with favor on the lowliness of his servant.
>> *Why is she lowly?*
> Surely, from now on all generations will call me blessed;
>> *Blessed for what?*
> for the Mighty One has done great things for me,
>> *Why is God the "Mighty One"?*
> and holy is his name.
> His mercy is for those who fear him
>> *Why is it important to fear God?*
> from generation to generation
> He has shown strength with his arm;
>> *To whom does he show strength?*
> He has scattered the proud
>> *Who are proud in thought?*
> in the thoughts of their hearts.
> He has brought down the powerful from their thrones
>> *Who are the powerful?*
> and lifted up the lowly;
>> *Who are the lowly?*
> he has filled the hungry with good things,
>> *Who are the hungry?*
> and sent the rich away empty.

Who are the rich?
He has helped his servant Israel,
in remembrance of his mercy,
What is the mercy that's remembered?
according to the promise he made to our ancestors,
to Abraham and to his descendants forever.
What is the promise?

The Rev. Dawn Hutchings makes the following summary point about the Magnificat: "Mary is being clearly established as a revolutionary hero-ine, in a nationalistic and violent tradition. And the Magnificat is a song of revolution which proclaims the downfall of the prevailing order. The Mag-nificat is a rallying cry to overturn the established order of wealth; a tune intended to rouse the troops."[6] Most of Christian thought seems to focus on the early verses in which Mary is overcome by the Holy Spirit, leading to the idea of a non-biological conception with the implication of the "purity" of Mary. However, is purity the issue? Or is it justice? Hutchings writes: "In the later verses Mary could be thought to be a 'justice fighter' who calls for the justice of God."[7]

Finally, it is possible that the idea of Mary's purity in Jesus's conception by the Holy Spirit is not only bad biology but also bad theology. Certainly, a virgin birth is not consistent with a twenty-first-century biological view of human reproduction. And theologically, should purity be the focus of Christianity? Why does Mary need to be pure? She must be pure only if sin is related to sex.

Anglican priest Giles Frazer writes:

> That Mary's womb was "spotless" was perhaps a cover story de-signed by Jesus's supporters to explain a more God-like nature for his arrival. But here's the problem. For what separates Chris-tianity from other religious traditions is that . . . Christianity deliberately refuses the familiar distinction between the pure and the impure—Jesus was born in a cowshed. From lepers to prostitutes, he deliberately courted the ritually unclean. And he spent most of his ministry tearing down barriers between pure and impure—not least, those of the Temple—that separated the "ungodly" from God himself.
>
> In Christianity, purity is abolished. . . . Or, in other words, God is perfectly at home in a human life, with all its ritualistic mess, from blood to semen. There is no shame in the constitu-ent elements of our humanity, including the manner in which

6. Hutchings, "Pregnant with Possibility."

7. Hutchings, "Pregnant with Possibility."

we are made. Which is why the "pure virgin" tradition runs totally against the grain. The problem is not just basic biology: it doesn't add up theologically.[8]

Let's also keep in mind the issue of worldviews. Virgin births with no human father may be possible in the worldviews of Bible times up into the Middle Ages. However, they are problematic in terms of the cosmology and biology of the last four centuries. And, if the whole point of salvation is to heal broken or damaged systems in our lives today, stressing purity is bad theology. How can Jesus be a meaningful moral exemplar for humans if he himself is not human, if he is not born like us?

What kind of moral exemplar was Jesus? Was he an inspirational model for how we should treat others in our personal relationships? Within families? In our church? In our community? Certainly, all these systems are important. However, it is more than this. In the context of the Roman Empire, New Testament scholar Marcus Borg says that Jesus was a nonviolent revolutionary against Roman domination aided by Jewish leaders, who were a part of the Jerusalem temple. Jesus led a protest movement similar to those of Gandhi or Martin Luther King.

Whom did Jesus lead? If one looks at his followers whom he talked to about the coming of God's kingdom, whom he healed, and how he argued with wealthy, religious Jews (the Sadducees and the Pharisees), it becomes clear that the coming kingdom was of the poor and oppressed—the farmers, fishermen, construction workers, the sick, the despised tax collectors, prostitutes, and others. It was for the people of the land. So, he went about Galilee, just as Judas the Galilean had done. But instead of murdering and pillaging, Jesus healed the sick and spoke to those who suffered about the coming kingdom of God—in fact it was right here, where two or three had gathered, and for the thousands who followed him.

The climax of Jesus's nonviolent revolution was his leading his followers into Jerusalem. The Palm Sunday procession, the throwing the money changers out of the temple, the debates with Jewish leaders, all are actions of a nonviolent revolutionary who protested the Roman domination system on behalf of the poor and oppressed. Marcus Borg writes that "the opening act of this week is the Palm Sunday procession." This was not the only procession at that time. Each year at Passover, the Roman governor Pilate rode into Jerusalem with his armed forces from the west. He came from the governing city of Maritima on the Mediterranean coast to guard against things getting out of hand among the Jews. Jesus came into Jerusalem from the east. The biblical texts tell us that this was not accidental. It was a procession

8. Fraser, "Story of the Virgin Birth."

that Jesus had planned. According to Borg, "his decision to enter the city as he did was what we could call a planned political demonstration, a counter-demonstration. The juxtaposition of these two processions embodies the central conflict of Jesus's last week: the kingdom of God or the kingdom of imperial domination . . . two visions of life on earth."[9]

The Romans did not see Jesus as a peaceful, nonviolent resister. The large crowds that followed Jesus wherever he went were significant cause for concern. They may have thought of him like they thought of Judas the Galilean. So, with the help of Jewish leaders from the temple, they treated Jesus just like they had treated countless other political dissidents and protestors. They crucified him.

RESURRECTION

How can we understand Jesus's resurrection in a Christianity for this world only, the world informed by modern science? How can we understand it in a naturalistic worldview? Isn't the resurrection of Jesus supernatural?

To understand the resurrection in a naturalistic worldview, we have to return to the idea of God that I set out in the first chapter. God is "seen" when we look at the world in terms of its creative interactions. In terms of creative good rather than created good. That Jesus was born when Mary was raped by a Roman soldier was something that became a created good. Jesus as the leader of nonviolent resistance was also created good. However, Jesus's birth and life also can be viewed from the perspective of creativity. This is the perspective of looking at the *interactions* between Jesus and his disciples, between Jesus and those he taught, between Jesus and those he healed. The heart of these interactions was Jesus's love for everyone, regard-less of who they were. It was his living for justice for the poor, oppressed, and rejected. As the moral exemplar Jesus continues to live.

Henry Nelson Wieman thinks that everything is an event—an inter-action among a variety of parts in relationship. In the New Testament, the life of Jesus is told as a series of events. His parables also portray events. In such events Jesus catalyzed creative interchange with his disciples, which transformed them so that they became capable of such interchange among themselves. Immediately following the death of Jesus their interchange with him seemed to cease—only to return in a new way. During Jesus's life it had been limited in scope to its Jewish context. However, after his cru-cifixion creative love and justice broke forth in his disciples and overcame

9. Borg, *Jesus*, 232.

this cultural limitation to become available to the wider world, universal in its scope.[10]

This kind of event continues as the unconditional, undiscriminating loving that Jesus practiced during his life. It continues in the cry for justice for the poor and oppressed. People today participate in the Christ event (which they may call by other names) whenever they expand the boundaries of their communities, whenever they expand the circle of who is in the moral community with acts of compassion and justice for all. This brings salvation to an ever-wider number of systems. It heals brokenness and helps more systems, (individual, family, community, national, and international systems) dynamically function well. This is the heart of Christian Naturalism.

10. Wieman, *Source of Human Good*, 39–44, 278.

7

PRACTICING CHRISTIANITY

IN THIS BOOK, BEING Christian is not so much what we think or feel as what we do—as how we live. In chapter 5 I suggested that an appropriate theory of atonement (how to become united with God) for Christian naturalists is Peter Abelard's moral exemplar theory. The love Jesus exhibited in the New Testament Gospels acts as the inspirational model for how anyone who follows Jesus should live their lives. Developing this idea further, we will look to see how this idea of being in union with God helps us positively work and play with the "other." We will explore how in our Christian living we can follow Jesus and address problems of racism and sexism within ourselves, our church community, and our society, and how we can respond to speciesism and climate change on our planet.

THE PARABLE OF THE GOOD SAMARITAN

One of my favorite parables of Jesus is that of the Good Samaritan in Luke 10. It helps me understand whom I should love, and how I should love.

> Then a lawyer stood up to test Jesus. "Teacher," he said, "what must I do to inherit eternal life?" He said to him, "What is written in the law? What do you read there?" He answered, "You shall love the Lord your God with all your heart, and with all your soul, and with all your strength, and with all your mind; and your neighbor as yourself." And he said to him, "You have given the right answer; do this, and you will live."

But wanting to justify himself, he asked Jesus, "And who is my neighbor?" Jesus replied, "A man was going down from Jerusalem to Jericho, and fell into the hands of robbers, who stripped him, beat him, and went away, leaving him half dead. Now by chance a priest was going down that road; and when he saw him, he passed by on the other side. So likewise a Levite, when he came to the place and saw him, passed by on the other side. But a Samaritan while traveling came near him; and when he saw him, he was moved with pity. He went to him and bandaged his wounds, having poured oil and wine on them. Then he put him on his own animal, brought him to an inn, and said, 'Take care of him; and when I come back, I will repay you whatever more you spend.' Which of these three, do you think, was a neighbor to the man who fell into the hands of the robbers?" He said, "The one who showed him mercy." Jesus said to him, "Go and do likewise." (Luke 10:25–37)

I'd like to unpack some of the meaning of the two great commandments and the parable of the good Samaritan in the context of a naturalistic worldview. In particular I want to explore: What does it mean to love God completely, to love neighbor, and to love myself? Let's look at these in reverse order, beginning with myself. What am I, what should I love? In chapter 2, I answered this question in terms of a dynamic systems understanding, especially when I talked about the interaction between parts of the evolving brain.

WHAT AM I? I'M A COMMITTEE

When I began teaching at Rollins College, I experienced something quite new. I had experienced this before but not to the extent that I was experiencing it at Rollins. It was the experience of committees. After his or her first year of teaching, all faculty were expected to serve on one or more committees. And there were lots of committees. As I served on a couple of committees, I began to consider that my mind also could be regarded as a committee. It was a committee of teaching classes, counseling students, attending department meetings, considering issues raised at meetings of the college-wide curriculum committee. And, of course, there were faculty meetings—regular faculty meetings two or three times a term and emergency faculty meetings.

I remember late one afternoon in my office. Having finished teaching two classes, I had open-office hours for any student who wanted to drop by. But a part of me knew I had course preparation for the following day. Still other parts wanted to play tennis with Jack, a faculty colleague. Or "chew the fat" with department colleagues. I felt like a committee with several members—all wanting different things.

INTERNAL FAMILY SYSTEMS (IFS)

In the last fifteen years I've learned about a more nuanced understanding of my mind as a committee. It is a well-developed, tested, and quite useful understanding of our complex minds that are carried by our complex brains.

This understanding portrays the mind as consisting of internal systems and is based on a well-established approach to therapy called "family systems."

"Family systems theory is an approach to understanding human functioning that focuses on interactions between people in a family and between the family and the context(s) in which that family is embedded."[1] One form of this kind of therapy was developed by Murray Bowen in the 1950s. Bowen was a professor of clinical psychology at Georgetown University. In contrast to the then dominant Freudian theory of psychoanalysis that focused on the individual, Bowen followed the new systems thinking developed in computer science and applied analogously in a variety of fields. Applied to the family, the family is understood to be a complex social system in which members interact and influence each other's behavior. Because family members interact and interconnect, it is appropriate to view the system as a whole. "Any change in one individual within a family is likely to influence the entire system and may even lead to change in other members. Many interventions designed to promote behavior change in children are directed at the parent-child unit, although it may be more beneficial to focus on the family as a whole."[2]

Richard Schwartz, having earned a PhD in marriage and family systems theory, began working with his clients to help them experience themselves inwardly as a system consisting of sub-personalities or "parts."[3] Introspectively, viewing myself as an internal family system helps me to better experience what I am and what it means to *love myself*. And also, what it means to love other systems such as my neighbor, people in my society, and systems of species on planet earth. I'll share with you the types of some interactive parts that help our internal systems be effective. I'll also point

1. Watson, *Encyclopedia of Human Behavior*, 184–93.

2. Gilbertson and Graves, "Heart Health and Children."

3. I learned about this psychotherapeutic approach from my wife, Marj Davis, who often used it in her pastoral counseling. I used it with my own psychotherapist when I began grieving my loss of Marj after she died.

to some research of our physical brain systems that carry our subjectively experienced parts.

Internal family systems offers a guiding model to reach compassionate mindfulness of inner states and processes. Our inner family consists of several "sub-personalities" or "subsystems," or simply "parts." We can analyze them, first, as self and parts. Second, our parts are divided into protectors and exiles. Third, protectors consist of managers and firefighters. (See figure on the next page for more detail.)

SELF	PARTS
PROTECTORS	EXILES
MANAGERS	FIREFIGHTERS

All our sub-personalities are valuable. It is likely that they have evolved into their various roles for our evolutionary survival in relation to the external environment and to other persons in our society. When not under stress, they work together harmoniously. They function well. However, under pressure, parts may be forced into extreme roles and try to take over the internal system.

The Internal System

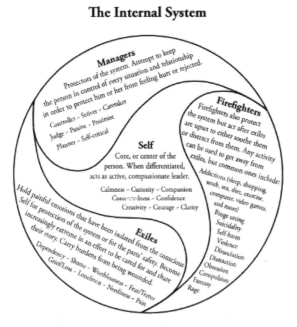

Fig. 34. The Internal System (Mullen 2001–2002), Text adapted from Richard C. Schwartz, Internal Family Systems Theory (1995), Graphic by Janet R. Mullen. Permission given by Janet R. Mullen.

LOVING MYSELF

In terms of IFS what does it mean to love ourselves? It means entering our core "self" and engaging our parts or sub-personalities with compassionate mindfulness. One way I think about the self is as the "I" that experiences things within myself, like remembering a dream or a book I've read, and also experiencing things outside myself. As I look out the window at the tree in my yard, I'm also able to include myself in the experience. I experience myself as subject in relation to experienced objects.

One should not think of the "self" as a kind of part. It is not a part but the underlying core of the "inner family." It is the inner experience of being in a calm, centered state, with full awareness in the present moment of all that is going on within and without. This same state of consciousness, called "being in self-leadership" and "self," is comparable with the notions of soul, spirit, sacred center, Buddha nature, atman (Hindu), mind of Christ, inner light (Quaker), the beloved (Sufi Islam), and others. For many, it has a profound spiritual quality.

When a person is in this state of self, she or he feels calm, connected, and compassionate, with a sense of curiosity, creativity, clarity, confidence, and courage. This state is sensed by the person and can also be sensed by others. While in this state of consciousness, called "self-leadership," the self can interact with various manager, firefighter, and exile parts and guide them to work together harmoniously, which helps a person like me or you to live more consciously and effectively.

SELF AND MEDITATION

The self is always present, but sometimes it can be "eclipsed" by parts in their extreme protective roles. The goal of therapy, or of going inward by ourselves often with the help of a healer (a therapist), is to bring all parts under the leadership of the self. This state of being in self in IFS is similar to what some psychologists and neuroscientists consider as two kinds of popular meditation—"mindfulness meditation" and "loving-kindness meditation." Here's my own integration of these two.

Both begin with posture. I sit in a chair that supports the straightness of my back, with feet flat on the floor. Next, I focus on my breathing. I slowly breath in and out and experience the air as it enters and exits my body.

In this calm state of breathing, I open myself up to experience my surroundings, sounds, smells, sitting in the chair, and other sensations. I simply observe them coming and going in and out of my awareness. I don't try to hold them in my mind. I'm mindful or aware of them, but I simply let them come and go.

Next, I become aware of the parts of my body. I begin with my feet and let go. I let my awareness move slowly up my legs, ankles, knees, hips, and buttocks. Each time letting the awareness come and go. Lovingly I thank them for all they do for me.

Then I move up the trunk of my body and become aware of it external-ly and internally. I express loving-kindness and thankfulness to these parts. I do the same as my awareness goes from my shoulders down and up my arms. Then I become aware, one at a time, of the various parts of my face, loving each part and thanking them for what they do for me. Finally, I move inside my head to observe various aspects of my consciousness—hearing words, seeing images, smells, feelings—letting each experience easily come and go. I accept them lovingly and thankfully let them go, until all fade away and the only experience I have is consciousness itself.

A simpler exercise for coming to be in self is given by Thich Nhat Han:

> Breathing in, I calm my body. Breathing out, I smile.
> Dwelling in the present moment, I know this is a wonderful moment.

He then shortens this to single words:

> As we breathe in, we say to ourselves, "Calming,"
> And as we breathe out, we say, "Smiling."
> As we breathe in again, we say, "Present moment,"
> and as we breathe out, "Wonderful moment."[4]

I and you are now in a state of loving or compassionate mindfulness of ourselves with all our parts. We are in what IFS calls self. In self we can become aware of our managers, exiles, and firefighters.

Managers

"Manager" parts are action programs of the brain that function to keep everything under control and working smoothly. They protect us by keep-ing us organized and "on track." Managers can be related to the "executive" functions of the prefrontal cortex connected to other parts of the brain such as the hyppocampus (working memory) and amygdala (motivation).[5]

4 Hanh, *Living Buddha*, 16.

5. Protectors (managers/firefighters) always have a job. When they are tasked with protecting the system from the pain (burden) of the exile, they too may also be consid-ered burdened—but they are burdened with their job to protect (versus being able to be in their natural role in a healthy, balanced system.). In ancient Israel, our managers

EXILES

Exiles are emotions and feelings that usually are shaped by painful inter-actions with the external world—often in childhood. Examples are pain, fear, shame, grief, "not good enough," and hopelessness. Despite the efforts of managers to keep them from being experienced (to keep them "in the closet"), exiles can sometimes be activated in stressful situations and act out in extreme ways. They act out in an effort to be recognized and cared for, like many who have been oppressed, imprisoned, or marginalized.

FIREFIGHTERS

When the managers are unable to control exiles and life becomes confused, other sub-personalities take over, often in extreme and even self-destructive ways. Examples are excessive eating, sleeping, sex, drinking, shopping, cut-ting oneself, drugs, and fantasy. The above circle diagram gives more detail.

RACIST, SEXIST, SPECIES-BIASED PARTS

Do I have racist, sexist, and species-biased parts? As I discussed in chapter 4 on "Human Evil," I live in a society of liberal, progressive, and Christian values. However, I wonder if I have parts that are in exile, hidden in my unconsciousness, but that emerge into the fringes of consciousness when I'm discussing these topics with others or avoid going to discussions. This unconscious hiddenness has been identified by some scientists as "implicit bias" against certain types of humans as well as certain types of life organ-isms. I can recognize them and with listening love help them as I am in introspective awareness—as I am "in self."

---

might have used the Ten Commandments to keep relationships organized. The manag-ers in the second half of the commandments set boundaries. As Huston Smith has pointed out: think of all the things you can do in relationship to your neighbor. But you can't kill him, have sex with his wife, steal from him, give false testimony, or desire anything that is his. The last is the most difficult, because it involves the emotional parts we experience inwardly in our brains. Not coveting is the "flip side" of loving your neighbor. The commandments setting boundaries unpack in part what loving your neighbor means.

BEING IN SELF

How does one come to be "in self"? As I've already said, one way is though mindfulness and loving-kindness meditation. However, I find it also occurs more immediately when I take a deep breath. Try taking five deep breaths. Each time, as I exhale, I feel myself relaxing more and more. I leave all thoughts behind and settle into a calm experience of being aware. At first it is for a few moments. But with a little practice, I can stay in this state longer and begin to "awaken" my parts. I bring a part, one at a time, to my centered awareness, listen with love to what they have to say, and perhaps discover why they carry racist, sexist, or speciesist feelings. I lovingly guide them to be more accepting of others as they engage with others.

Here is the experience of self as Schwartz describes it during and after a session with a client in therapy:

> Once you're attuned with your client, the session begins to flow, and there's an almost effortless quality to the work, as if something magical were unfolding almost by itself. I don't even think about what I'm going to say—the right words just come out, as if something were speaking through me. Afterward, I'm full of energy, as if I'd been meditating for an hour rather than doing hard, demanding, clinical work.
>
> In a sense, of course, I've been in a state of meditation— a state of deep mindfulness, full-bodied attention, centered awareness, and inner calm. And even after all these years, I still have the sense of being witness to something awe inspiring, as if the client and I both were connected to something beyond us, much bigger than we are.[6]

The self-to-self attunement described by Schwartz is one way of saying, "Love your neighbor *as yourself*." As we are "in self" we are open to all our parts in what I call "listening love," allowing them to share what is really going on with them. We love ourselves. And as we are in self with the selves of others, we are also in listening love with their exiles, their managers, and their firefighters.

LOVE YOUR NEIGHBOR—EMPATHY

There is a biological basis for our being able to love our neighbors. We have evolved with brains that are capable of empathy. There are three kinds of empathy. One is emotional, feeling what another person feels, like an echo

---

6. Schwartz, "Larger Self."

of their state in our own minds. Emotional empathy uses the amygdala, hippocampus, and insula.[7] A second is cognitive empathy, the ability to think how another person is thinking. The primary brain system for this is the prefrontal cortex. Pathways of neurotransmitters such as dopamine and serotonin enable connections with parts of the limbic system A third kind of empathy is compassion. Out of emotional and cognitive empathy a person shows and acts with compassion to help others.

Brain systems that underlie empathy evolved when you and I were hunter-gatherers living on the African savannas. Natural selection favored empathy toward others in our extended family or tribe. However, we did not develop as strong a biologically based empathy toward groups of humans outside our own family. Established through evolution was an insider-outsider division.

One example of how this works involves the hormone oxytocin. Called the "love hormone," oxytocin enables strong bonding between a mother and her baby—mother love. Oxytocin is also involved to a lesser extent in loving relations between mother and father, and other family members. However, studies also show that it is present with increased suspicion, feelings of hostility, and defensive aggression toward outsiders—those who are not members of "our tribe."[8]

So, the evolution of our brains gave rise to empathy—a biological basis of love. But natural selection also established the insider-outsider division among different groups of humans. An extremely important question is whether the love of Jesus can inspire a love of neighbor that overcomes this division.

WHO IS MY NEIGHBOR?

"Who is my neighbor?" the rich young man asked in the good Samaritan parable. In answer to this I'd like to remind us of what I said in chapter 4 about the moral community. Based on my sketching our journey as part of the journey of all things—from our being hydrogen atoms to our present state as members of species *Homo sapiens* on planet earth, I would say we are all neighbors. Actually, we are all family. Also, as humans with our "big brains," we are family inside our brains and bodies. Or we might say that in our internal family system, each part is a neighbor to other parts guided by a core experience of our being called self. So, I'm to love my neighbor across my street as I love my own complex person named Karl Peters. Also, I should

7. See Goleman and Davidson, *Altered Traits.*

8. Badcock, "Imprinted Brain."

love all humans as I love Karl Peters—and *all other species, ecosystems, and even the planet*. How can I do this? It seems impossible. One strategy I've learned is *to listen*, to listen to all my neighbors (listening includes using the other senses as well). I call this being in a state of "listening love."

This is the state that Thich Nhat Han describes in the following passage: he points out that being in a calm, centered state, in the present moment without conflict, also enables us to love others. "When we are mindful, touching deeply the present moment, we can see and listen deeply, and the fruits are always understanding, acceptance, love, and the desire to relieve suffering and bring joy. When our beautiful child comes up to us and smiles, we are completely there for her."[9] Completely there for our child. Completely there for our neighbor. Listening love.

A second way extends listening love more formally. It is "loving kindness meditation."[10] Sometimes this is called "compassion meditation." In compassion meditation one allows feelings of loving warmth to arise in one's awareness, welcoming all feelings, thoughts, and sensations without judgment as they flow in and out of attention. Both mindfulness and loving-kindness meditation may elicit ongoing changes in the brain areas such as the left and right amygdala, parts which are important in emotions.[11]

NEIGHBORS IN A CHURCH COMMUNITY

Some years ago, I asked my minister why people came to our local church. He replied that there are three reasons. First, people come, usually to the minister, because they are in crisis. As they are helped, they think about exploring more of what goes on. Sometimes they become members. Second, middle-age adults come with their children because they want their girls and boys to have a religious education, especially an education in values to live by. Third, people come as they get older, hoping to become a part of a community that can provide morale and physical support to sustain them until death. They also have talents they can share with others.

Jesus provides a similar insight. Note how physical he is in the New Testament Gospels. As a moral exemplar he shows us how to live a Christian life? He tells us to reach out to help people in need: feed the hungry, give drink to the thirsty, welcome the stranger, provide clothing to those in need, look after the sick, and visit those in prison (Matt 25:34–35). And notice

---

9. Hanh, *Living Buddha*, 14.

10. Goleman and Davidson, *Altered Traits*, 109–12.

11. Desbordes et al., "Effects of Mindful-Attention and Compassion Meditation Training."

how he himself lived the kingdom of God that was at hand. The kinds of people he associated with are just as important an example for us as what he did for them: fishermen, working-class people of whom he was one, tax collectors (in league with the Jerusalem leaders and the Romans), women, the sick, people possessed by demons. Would we want to associate with this Jesus today? Are these kinds of people in our own local churches? Are all part of our welcoming congregations?

A NON-WELCOMING CONGREGATION

How should we welcome strangers? What we should *not* do is the following:

When I first moved to the Hartford area, I was living alone. One Sunday I decided to go to church. I was cordially welcomed at the entrance before the service and asked to sign the guest book. In the sanctuary I sat halfway to the front. A lot of people were there. The choir was excellent. The minister gave a thought-provoking sermon. And after church I followed the flow of a large crowd to the social hour for coffee and conversation.

The room reminded me of a gymnasium. I got my coffee at one end. Then I went out to the center, and stood waiting for someone to come up, say hello, and engage me in conversation. I stood there, and I stood there, and I stood there. No one came up to me. Finally, an older man walked up with his coffee, and we talked. As we talked, I learned he was a minister. I thought to myself, "He doesn't count!" I never went back to that church. I felt like a stranger who was not "taken in."

The incident reminded me, in contrast, of my first visit to a church in Orlando, Florida. It was 1983, ten years after Carol and I moved to central Florida, and we thought we should become part of a community of people who shared our beliefs and values. We had just stepped in the door, into a crowd of people, and someone came up to us, asked who we were, told us about the church, and introduced us to other people. Even though we were not hungry, thirsty, poorly clothed, sick, or in prison, my wife and I were strangers—and we were welcomed! After some years passed, I became president of this welcoming congregation.

LOOKING FOR STRANGERS

Because of these experiences, I have always been on the lookout for strangers or people I don't know. At the church I currently attend, during the social hour after the service, I'll go up to someone I haven't seen before who is standing alone. (These often are men.) After introducing ourselves, we share how we came to be at this place. And I make sure I introduce them to one of our ministers and some others from the congregation. The following Sundays I look for the same person. Each time we get to know each other a little better. Eventually one man joined our church and another shared his musical talent by performing during some worship services.

Doing this I did have one experience that was embarrassing. One Sunday I saw a man across the social hall, alone. I went up to him and said, "I'm Karl Peters; I haven't seen you before." He responded by introducing himself, and then he said, "Oh, I've been here for some time. My kids are in the Christian Education program, and I always help out there. These are my kids," as a girl and a boy came up to us. "Time for me to take them home."

Briefly, I felt humiliated, but then I realized that this has happened in every church I have attended in the past fifty years. People with children, young and middle-aged parents, make up a very large group of those involved in churches. They come with their children for the first part of the service. The children hear a story just for them from a minister or worship leader. Then they leave the service, often with their parents, who help teach the kids in the Sunday School. In contrast, older, retired folks regularly attend church, and even though they enjoy hearing the story told to children and singing them to their classes, we don't often get to know them or their parents. It's very easy to remain strangers to one another.

LOVING OUR NEIGHBOR IN CONNECTION CIRCLES

When I went to church alone, I often sat by myself. Gradually I came to know a person in my pew and two people behind me. I enjoyed the service, especially the choir and the sermon. I also enjoyed singing some of the hymns, even though I sometimes found the theology outdated. However, even with everything happening in the service, I felt like I was in a crowd and not a congregation. Sometimes it felt like a "lonely crowd." So, when I heard about a new program called "Connection Circles," I decided to try it out. These small groups of eight to ten adults are designed to help us share ourselves with one another. They usually meet for eight weeks. They encourage listening love.

These groups are present in different denominations. Besides being called "Connection Circles," they might be called "Small Group Ministry," "Covenant Groups," "Caring Groups," or simply "Small Groups." I liked the idea of "connection circles," because it suggested some possible growth in loving one's neighbor.[12]

12. The following is an example of a connection circle session at the Unitarian Society of Harford. It was given to me by a friend, Bill Shoemaker.

I was excited when I saw the list of topics for the current eight-week groups. It was on the theme of disability. After an introductory meeting each session considered a particular topic: (1) Becoming Disabled; (2) In My Chronic Illness I Found a Deeper Meaning; (3) Disabled, Shunned, and Silenced in America; (4) Listening as a Sacred Art; (5) Depression Is Agony. Just Ask Jason Kander—or Me; (6) Resilience; and (7) A World of Our Own.

I signed up for one of the six groups available. There were ten in my group. We met for two hours, one evening a week, in the home of the host member of the group. He or she took care of the beverages, and the rest of us brought snacks. Some of us loaded our plates at the beginning and intermission. Usually only one member of a family attends a connection circle. Parents with children may each attend on different evenings, and for a Friday evening or Saturday group there may be a separate program for children and infant-toddler care.

When I signed up, I and everyone else in all the groups were given the following covenant. The covenant stated the details of our commitment and the way we were supposed to conduct our meetings.

As members of this Connection Circle, we covenant with one another to help make this experience we are sharing both personally and spiritually rewarding for one another, to nourish our sense of community, and to learn and practice right relationship.

We will try to arrive well before the beginning of each meeting, so that the meeting can start on time and so that the meeting is not disrupted by late arrivals.

- During the check-in, we will do our best to share briefly and in the present tense the things that are most intensely in our minds and hearts as we arrive.

- We will do our best to:

- allow one person to speak at a time;

- speak about *our own* personal feelings and experiences rather than about our abstract opinions or the feelings and experiences of others or people in general—this process involves sharing events or stories in our lives and relating how they have personally affected us;

- allow a moment of silence after the previous person stops speaking before beginning to speak ourselves, because this shows respect for the speaker *and* gives us time to absorb the possible meanings their words may have for us, and;

- help ensure that *everyone* has time to share by being aware of how long and how often we speak.

- When others are sharing, we will do our best to give them our undivided and silent attention, rather than mentally formulating a response or rehearsing what we will say next.

- Strict confidentially is required. We will not disclose information shared by other group members unless we have their clear permission, and we will not name the participants to anyone outside of the group.

Each week before our next meeting, all six connection circles were given the same reading and a set of questions to guide our reflection and provide starting points for sharing. Here's a sample of the material for one of our sessions. Even if we have read it before the meeting, it is also read out loud at the beginning.

"LISTENING AS A SACRED ART," BY ALICE A. HOLSTEIN

My experiences suffering with bipolar mood disorder include some dramatic examples, partly because I lived sometimes on the streets when I was really sick. . . . One of those times was after I had been released from the hospital after a manic episode. Upon discharge, they did not ask me where I would be staying, and I was still somewhat delusional, so I did not have the capacity to think clearly for myself. I was on foot, without such things as credit cards or money.

The night (in La Crosse, WI) was chilly and rainy. I knew I needed help, but newly arrived in my hometown after 40 years absence, did not know how to meet that need. After stopping at one place where there was "no room at the inn," I was referred down the street to St. Rose Convent late in the evening. Fortunately, they let me in through their locked door and then they called one of the Franciscan Sisters to the receiving room. Immediately I told her that I thought I was going to die. . . .

The nun just listened to me. She did not try to talk me out of that story, nor to give advice. She merely listened with careful attention, holding my hand at one point and praying with me. She had no solution to my dilemma of a place to stay, but I was somehow strengthened enough to go back out into the rainy night and make my way to a Catholic Worker house nearby. It was closed, but there was a small children's playhouse in the backyard where I curled up and fell asleep. The next morning, when they opened, I proceeded to use their phone to begin making arrangements for temporary housing. I was restored enough to health to begin making rational decisions about how to help myself.

Listening, without judgement, with compassion and love, is a sacred art. . . . Whenever I was just listened to in such a way, I was validated and able to "return to my normal self" more quickly. I think we have hundreds of opportunities to listen effectively in a day or a week, but seldom do we realize how healing and life-giving that can be. . . . When have you been the recipient of such a gift? How well do you give it to others?[13]

After the reading we began sharing our own experiences, guided by questions like the following:

1. Remember a time when you felt you were not being listened to. How did it make you feel?

2. Remember a time when you felt someone listened intently to you. How did it make you feel?

3. Share a time when you wish you had listened more carefully.

4. What do you think the author meant when she said, "Listening is a sacred art"?

5. If you wish you were a better listener, what's keeping you from doing that?

Building a community in which everyone expands the circle of empathy by engaging others with listening love is not just following the commandment, love your neighbor as yourself. Through listening love from one individual to another, some who are strangers—outsiders to us—a new and vibrant system is created as part of a local congregation. It is a system that becomes empowered to follow Jesus out into the wider world.

13. Holstein, "Listening as a Sacred Art."

8

INTO THE WORLD

SOME TIME AGO MY minister raised the question in his sermon, "Where is Jesus today?" He wanted to move us beyond thinking about the historical Jesus, about Jesus in the Bible, to considering how Jesus—the Holy Spirit of Jesus—is in our church today. As he was talking an image arose in my mind—of Jesus coming forward from the cross into the chancel, and then moving from the front of the church down the center aisle. I thought that in the spirit of non-discriminating love he might then spread throughout the congregation. However, Jesus did not stop with the congregation. He kept moving to the back of the sanctuary and then right out the front door. I felt his call: "Come and follow me."

Many Christians today are concerned about the decline in attendance. Certainly, some in my local church are. We wonder, if the decline continues, will we be able to continue as a viable local congregation?

According to social scientist Robert Putnam, this decline has been part of a decline of groups throughout our society. In *Bowling Alone* he tells of the decline of *all* groups since World War II. During the war, the United States became extensively united, and after the war membership in groups was the highest it had ever been anytime during the twentieth century.

Fig. 35. Lady Bowling Alone. License: CC0 Public Domain.

What happened? *Television.* Television came into the market in the late 1940s. From 1945 to 1960 the number of households with television sets grew dramatically. In 1945 there were probably fewer than ten thousand TV sets in the country. By 1950 there were about six million. In 1960 there were almost sixty million, and in 2006 there were 285 million in use in United States households.[1]

The impact on family life was huge. When I was a teenager in the '50s, I remember the invention of TV dinners, eaten on TV tables, in front of the television set. There were no longer family discussions of the events of the day around a dining room or kitchen table. Even together in the living room or family room, everyone was watching TV. Each person was alone.

In 1954 my father took me sixty miles from our home to Milwaukee to see a major league baseball game—the Milwaukee Braves. Being at a real live game was the experience of the decade for me. However, I didn't need to attend live games. I could watch major league baseball on television, and also major league football and basketball—all by myself. I was "bowling alone." Back then professional sports were essentially male, played by men and watched by men. We were part of a "virtual" men's club in which no one knew anyone else.

So, it is likely that the decline in church attendance is part of a larger decline because human activity came to be defined by television. But not only television! It has been also defined by the emergence of new groups. Community theater groups. Artist Way groups. Bird watching groups, hiking groups. There are also sports groups for young men and women from

1. Lefky and Tamazasvili, "Number of Televisions in the US."

grade school through high school. The activities of many of these groups occur on weekends. Sometimes they impact directly on churches and on Sunday mornings. My church moved its worship services to an earlier time, so that families with children playing in a Sunday soccer league could come to church, go home, and then get ready to play their games.

What I wonder is this. Jesus has gone out the church door into the wider world. Is his spirit embedded in soccer rules of fair play, in teamwork, in winning and losing graciously? What values do young people's formal group activities embody? Are they consistent with Christian values? Are Christian values already influential in various parts of the wider culture? Should churches embrace these activities instead of regarding them as competition? Can local congregations support the work of Jesus in the wider world? I think they should, they can, and sometimes they do.

LOVE AND JUSTICE

There are other people in the good Samaritan parable. There are those who pass by the man who was robbed, and there are the robbers. Are we supposed to love the robbers? Not necessarily. An appropriate response to the robbers is not love, but justice. Jesus is not only an exemplar of non-discriminating love. He also is an exemplar of justice.

As we have seen in chapters 5 and 6, Jesus lived in a powerful domination system—the Roman Empire. The country in which he lived, Palestine, was about ten thousand square miles, approximately 175 miles from north to south, or about the size of New Hampshire.[2] In contrast the Roman Empire was almost 1.7 million square miles and stretched from what is now England to India. The Jewish priests and scribes were agents of the empire in Palestine. They were trying to accommodate Rome to keep their own leadership positions and probably their lives. They too were part of the Roman domination system.

Jesus was different. He was on the side of those who were oppressed. He did not engage in revolutionary violence as Judas of Galilee and other zealots did. He taught and healed the poor, uneducated, and diseased, and he gathered a large following. With physical nonviolence he challenged the Jerusalem leaders and the empire. Marcus Borg, a prominent New Testament scholar, identifies Jesus as a "nonviolent religious revolutionary" demonstrating for justice.[3]

2. Barnes, "Bible Lands Notes," 1.

3. See Borg, *Jesus: Uncovering the Life, Teachings, and Relevance of a Religious Revolutionary.* However, Reza Aslan in *Zealot* makes the case that Jesus was part of the

So, how can we follow Jesus into the world, seeking justice in today's domination systems. Let's focus first on our current domination systems of racism and sexism. Later we'll look at the human worldwide domination system of earth's natural world. (Further descriptions of racism, sexism, and speciesism can be found in chapter 4.)

RACISM—INDIVIDUAL EFFORTS

I speculate: if Jesus lived among us today, how would he be treated based on the color of his skin? Jesus wasn't white! Being born and growing up in an eastern Mediterranean environment he would have had more melanin, and his skin color would be darker. And, since he and his father were carpenters, Jesus might even be found amid construction workers. Because the contemporary sciences have been advancing, it is possible for forensic anthropologists to construct a face of Jesus from a variety of data. This is what Richard Neave, a medical artist did in producing the above picture that was first published in the December 2002 issue of *Popular Mechanics* and republished in the April 2020 issue.

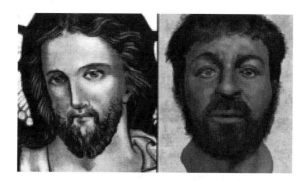

Fig. 36. White Jesus—Jewish Jesus: Reconstructing Jesus: Using Science to Flesh Out the Face of Religion, Liz Leafloor, Ancient Origins, December 16, 2015.

However, much of the Western visual art depicting Jesus most likely reinforces implicit white privilege found throughout the western part of the "Christian world."[4] This is in spite of the fact that earth includes many races that have their own images of Jesus.

history of warlike zealots. This is worth considering. One wonders, however, what kind of exemplar Jesus would be for today.

4. See *Wikipedia*, s.v. "Head of Christ," last modified January 11, 2022, https://en.wikipedia.org/wiki/Head_of_Christ.

WHITE PRIVILEGE

The first time I heard the words *white privilege* was from my good friend Jim. For several years Jim and I had weekly lunches. One noon he said to me, "Karl, I never thought of myself as having white privilege. Now I understand what it is, and I see how I could act like I have it. Last week I was in a department store and observed two women coming up to a jewelry counter, empty of customers. The black woman got to the counter first. About thirty seconds later a white woman came. The clerk walked over to the white woman and said, 'Can I help you?'" My friend continued, "Karl, if I hadn't had that class last week at church, I probably wouldn't even have noticed. But I did, and it really bothered me. I'll be more sensitive to other people, and I be on guard, watching myself when I might take preferential treatment when others should go first."

Jon Greenberg enlarges my friend's observation in an essay in *Yes* magazine:

> A white person's whiteness has come—and continues to come— with an array of benefits and advantages not shared by many people of color.

1. *The Privilege of Having a Positive Relationship with the Police, Generally*

2. *Of Being Favored by School Authorities*

3. *Of Attending Segregated Schools of Affluence*

4. *Of Learning about "My" Race in School*

5. *Of Finding Children's Books That Overwhelmingly Represent My Race*

6. *Of Soaking in Media Blatantly Biased toward My Race*

7. *Of Escaping Violent Stereotypes Associated with My Race*

8. *Of Playing the Colorblind Card, Wiping the Slate Clean of Centuries of Racism*

9. *Of Being Insulated from the Daily Toll of Racism*

10. *Of Living Ignorant of the Dire State of Racism Today.*[5]

5. Greenberg, "10 Examples."

RACISM: JUSTICE AND THE LAW

As I and you become aware of and work on our white bias, we and others in our church communities can support the wider effort of using the law to bring about justice. One very well-known racial justice organization is the Southern Poverty Law Center (SPLC), founded in 1971 as a civil rights law firm by Morris Dees, Joseph J. Levin Jr., and Julian Bond. "It is known for its legal cases against white supremacist groups, its classification of hate groups and other extremist organizations, and for promoting tolerance education programs."[6]

Ironically, in 2019 it also became known publicly for the reported sexual advances and sometimes inappropriate racial remarks by its founder, Dees. There also was a division between the jobs held by women and by men. Mostly women were in the lower-paid positions as secretaries, researchers, and filers for men, who were in higher, better-paid positions.

One employee has said, "We were working with a group of dedicated and talented people, fighting all kinds of good fights, making life miserable for the bad guys. And yet, all the time, dark shadows hung over everything: the racial and gender disparities, the whispers about sexual harassment, the abuses that stemmed from the top-down management, and the guilt you couldn't help feeling about the legions of donors who believed that their money was being used, faithfully and well, to do the Lord's work in the heart of Dixie. We were part of the con, and we knew it."[7]

However, since 2019 the SPLC has reorganized. Drees was fired. Richard Cohen, the president, resigned. Women and minorities are now in the top positions. The fifteen-member board of directors includes seven women and six people of color. The ten-member executive team, led by president and CEO Margaret Huang, includes seven women and five people of color.[8]

There also are other organizations without an ambiguous past reputation. One is Lawyers for Good Government (L4GG), founded in 2016 by Harvard Law School graduate Tracie Feit Love. Love has law experience at DLA Piper LLP and almost twenty years of experience "providing communications, digital marketing, and consulting services" to law firms. She used social media to bring together and organize more than 125,000 lawyers, law students, and activists to fight for Constitutional, civil, and human rights.

---

6. See *Wikipedia*, s.v. "Southern Poverty Law Center," last modified February 20, 2022, https://en.wikipedia.org/wiki/Southern_Poverty_Law_Center.

7. Moser, "Reckoning of Morris Dees."

8. See the SPLC staff page, https://www.splcenter.org/about/staff.

"L4GG has pro bono projects across the country in the areas of immigrants' rights, climate change, racial justice, and COVID."[9]

Another organization that addresses black civil rights and the rights of all people is Amnesty International, USA. Originating in 1961 it has become the "world's largest grassroots human rights organization," working to protect people wherever justice, freedom, truth, and dignity are denied, and someone's human rights is denied. Amnesty International's *priority campaigns* are (1) free people from ICE detention, (2) gun violence and a human rights crisis, and (3) refugee and migrant rights to ensure that people can rebuild their lives safely. *Priority issues* are (1) abolish the death penalty in the United States and worldwide, (2) expose and help end torture and other human rights violations, (3) expose and help stop unlawful killing by police, (4) protect people on the front lines defending all or our rights, (5) protect the rights of women, LGBT people, and Indigenous communities, (6) help free people imprisoned for exercising their human rights, (7) advocate ending Greenhouse Gas Emissions through a just transition to green energy, (8) ask what our fundamental rights look like in the digital age, and (9) fight for human rights on Capitol Hill, in the White House, and in the federal government.[10]

Do these organizations embody the spirit of Jesus? Should Christian churches recognize that these are places where Jesus is today and follow him here? A decline in church attendance could be offset by those—whether or not they call themselves Christians—who exhibit empathic love and seek justice in the so-called secular society. Doing what Jesus did!

MALE PRIVILEGE (SEXISM)

I've been an active member of the Institute on Religion in an Age of Science (IRAS) since 1972. In some ways IRAS is an egalitarian institution. Its annual conferences have occasionally dealt with agism, women in science and religion, and challenges to science and religion from the LGBTQ communities. However, in the forty-five conferences I've attended, there always has been an issue between the women and men. Men take over discussions, whether in response to speakers, in small groups, or in committee meetings. In recent years the chairs of plenary sessions have tried to make sure that women are recognized as much as men. But, unless some controlled guidance is given, the default situation is that men dominate discussions.

9. See their website, https://www.lawyersforgoodgovernment.org/.

10. See Amnesty International's website, https://www.amnestyusa.org.

I confess that I've been guilty of exercising male privilege. If there is no control, I jump right in. And probably stay involved longer than most. As I look around the lecture hall or committee room, I see women beginning to try to move into the discussion. But it is still difficult to crack the masculine bias. Most men seem to feel they are entitled to take the lead and hold on to it as long as they can.

As we'll see below an extreme form of male privilege is rape—dominating others against their will.

SPECIES PRIVILEGE

The great modern philosopher René Descartes argued that only humans have consciousness, because only humans have immaterial souls. If animals seem to be conscious, they are just sophisticated machines—what today we might call droids.[11] Animals can do unusual and amazing things—like fly. But we can shoot them down and eat them—fair game. They have no rights and can be used to feed humans, help plow fields, and provide hunting entertainment. We don't respect the value they have in just being alive.

I suggest that treating animals *only* as resources for food, work, or entertainment is speciesism. This is one of the roots of our environmental crises, including climate change. An important example is raising cattle for human consumption. In their process of digesting grass and gains, cattle release methane. Methane is a greenhouse gas that is much more potent than carbon dioxide. Over one hundred years methane has a global warming potential twenty-eight to thirty-six times that of carbon dioxide.[12]

LOVE AND JUSTICE FOR EARTH

First, let's recognize that the question "Who is my neighbor?" when considered in the context of cosmic, biological, and cultural evolution, is another way of asking, "Who is in the moral community?" This is how we asked the question in chapter 4. I suggested that being in the moral community is based on the current scientific understanding that we and everything else on earth began as hydrogen atoms three hundred thousand years after the initial inflation called the "big bang." Everything is interrelated in an evolving cosmic, biological, and on earth cultural community. Everything that has been created out of continuing creative interactions is a neighbor at a

11. See Kaldas, "Descartes versus Cudworth."

12. EPA, "Understanding Global Warming Potentials," para. 4.

particular time and place to other things that have been and are being created. This means that creatures like us, who can engage in conscious reflection about what we should do in the future, should consider that all existing things are our neighbors. This is the same as saying that every created good is a member of the moral community.

What? Does this mean that I should consider everything as worthy of "listening love," worthy of "really listening love"? Does it mean that, like people in the medical professions, I should do no harm? Does this mean that, as much as I am able, I should leave things be and appreciate them as they are? *Yes!* Like me, they have come forth as the result of the complex creativity of our cosmos. This is the attitude expressed in the following sonnet by my friend and fellow professor at Rollins College Alan Nordstrom. He titles it "Mighty Mite":

> This tiny flying insect shares the lamp
> I use at 3 a.m. to read and write,
> and I resist my rash impulse to stamp
> it with my thumb, put out its little light
> for what? Because he flits and vexes me?
> Because he busily scours the chair arm next
> to me or courts the bulb distractingly?
> What right do I have to crush his little ec-
> stasy by exercising might at whim?
> My magnifying glass brings him to view:
> One wing's askew. Is he all right? So flim-
> sy, delicate, precise, and living, too
> Yes, there he goes, a-whir again, aloft,
> mighty enough to turn one hard heart soft.[13]

Like Nordstrom, I too engage in listening love by leaving things alone. If I find a fly or a wasp buzzing at my window trying to get outside, I don't kill it. I trap it in a plastic container, slip a piece of a magazine cover between the container and the window, and then carry it outside and release it. After all, like me, it has taken 13.8 billion years for that creature to come to be. The same with spiders in my bathtub. I lightly surround them with a piece of tissue and take them to a safer place. When I lived in Florida, I did the same with cockroaches. Social insects are more of a problem. When a potato chip falls on the carpet and I don't see it, ants find it. The ants love the chips so much that by the next morning, a black mound has risen up from the floor—an ant Tower of Babel. Regrettably, I put out baited, pet-safe traps, only where I've seen ants. The point is to let things be as much as possible,

---

13. This poem was received in a personal communication with Nordstrom.

appreciating what they are as parts of our cosmic family—to give them a form of listening love.

The following story by feminist philosopher Karen Warren serves as a modern parable about how we benefit by being lovingly interrelated with our natural environment.

> From my very first rock climbing experience, I chose a some-what private spot, away from other climbers and on-lookers. After studying "the chimney," I focused all my energy on making it to the top. I climbed with intense determination, using whatever strength and skills I had to accomplish this challenging feat. By midway I was exhausted and anxious. I couldn't see what to do next—where to put my hands or feet. Growing increasingly more weary as I clung somewhat desperately to the rock, I made a move. It didn't work. I fell. There I was, dangling midair above the rocky ground below, frightened but terribly relieved that the belay rope had held me. I knew that I was safe. I took a look up at the climb that remained. I was determined to make it to the top. With renewed confidence and concentration, I finished the climb to the top.
>
> On my second day of climbing, I rappelled down about 200 feet from the top of the Palisades at Lake Superior to just a few feet above the water level. I could see no one—not my belayer, not the other climbers, no one. I unhooked slowly from the rappel rope and took a deep cleansing breath. I looked all around me—really looked—and listened. I heard a cacophony of voices—birds, trickles of water on the rock before me, waves lapping against the rocks below. I closed my eyes and began to feel the rock with my hands—the cracks and crannies, the raised lichen and mosses, the almost imperceptible nubs that might provide a resting place for my fingers and toes when I began to climb. At that moment I was bathed in serenity. I began to talk to the rock in an almost inaudible, child-like way, as if the rock were my friend. I felt an overwhelming sense of gratitude for what it offered me—a chance to know myself and the rock differently, to appreciate unforeseen miracles like the tiny flowers growing in the even tinier cracks in the rock's surface, and to come to know a sense of *being in relationship* with the natural environment. It felt as if the rock and I were silent conversational partners in a longstanding friendship. I realized then that I had come to care about this cliff which was so different from me, so unmovable and invincible, independent and seemingly indifferent to my presence. I wanted to be with the rock as I climbed. Gone was the determination to conquer the rock, to forcefully impose my

will on it; I wanted simply to work respectfully with the rock as I climbed. And as I climbed, that is what I felt. I felt myself *caring* for this rock and feeling thankful that climbing provided the opportunity for me to know it. and myself in this new way.[14]

In the framework of Christian thinking nested in our contemporary scientific worldview, Warren illustrates a remarkable expansion of Jesus's answer to the question from the rich young ruler, "Who is my neighbor?" There also is the unexpected twist at the end of the good Samaritan parable. Instead of asking, "Who is my neighbor," Jesus asks, "Who was the neighbor to" the man who was beaten and left for dead? It was a Samaritan. At that time, among the Jews living in Judea, the southern kingdom, Samaritans were anathema. They were not neighbors, but enemies. Jesus's example of the Samaritan as a loving neighbor suggests that we too can find such examples. We can look outside our usual circles of care for models of what it means to love as Jesus loved. Jesus has walked out of the doors of Christian churches and is present whenever anyone exhibits listening love that sees and responds to those in need. And those who respond to need may themselves be hungry, thirsty, strangers, naked, sick, in prison. Even the least of these, the poor and oppressed may be exemplars—followers of the way of Jesus.

GROUPS OF PEOPLE WHO LOVE THEIR NEIGHBORS

Certainly, I/you can love neighbors directly or indirectly by supporting others who love neighbors.

In my local church and community, I and you can work with others growing food in the church garden, providing community meals for those who suffer hardship and homelessness. We can help build positive race and gender relations, helping others tell their stories, educating the children and youth, visiting the elderly and the infirmed, working locally in Habitat for Humanity, providing inspiring entertainment through a local community theater, and providing for the well-being of other species within and outside our homes.

I can do the same kinds of things in my town and my region. I can financially support the loving, healing, dignifying work of others. I can live and love in ever-widening circles of care, ever more extensive environments of plant and animal habitats, helping more and more members of the moral community.

14. Warren, "Power and the Promise."

Those who follow Jesus don't need to name themselves Christians. Expressing love in action *is* being Christian, whether or not one identifies with the name.

SYSTEMIC LOVE

When we expand our thinking about Christian love to include ever larger systems, not just family and community systems, but countries with complex political, economic, and social systems nurtured by even larger ecosystems, how we can love our neighbors becomes significantly more complex. This is especially difficult when we are living in a very large domination system. As I've already said, a domination system occurs when one part of the system takes over to the detriment of other parts. For example, when emotions like anger take over my brain, other emotions and patterns of rational thought are sidelined and become less effective. Another example is a local church where one or two individuals take over control of a committee. I remember when the chair of a church's buildings and grounds committee came to meetings not only with a detailed agenda but with all the required decisions made in advance. The chair was no longer guiding an interactive group. The chair had taken over. The committee had become a "domination system."

On a much larger scale, our discussions in chapter 4 of racism, sexism, and speciesism were really discussions about domination systems. It's relatively easy to change small-scale domination systems—in our brains and within church committees—but how does one take on systemic evil and follow Jesus's command to love our neighbors as ourselves?

Perhaps by doing something like the following. First, a person, committee, or local church may "listen" to what is being done on a large scale. One example is the #BlackLivesMatter movement, which was founded in 2013 after George Zimmerman was acquitted of Trayvon Martin's murder in Sanford, Florida. The #BLM movement was reinvigorated by the horrible murder of George Floyd by Minneapolis police officer Derek Chauvin. Chauvin stood with his knee on Floyd's neck for nine minutes until Floyd could no longer breath. Chauvin snuffed the life out of Floyd. This was recorded by video cameras that spread the killing via the internet around the world. In the United States a protest erupted first in Minneapolis and then in cities and towns around the country.

In my small town of Granby, Connecticut, citizens were organized by a businesswoman with the help of ministers and their churches. White people stood on both sides of a main street with large signs "Black Lives Matter." As cars drove between the displayed signs, many honked their horns in support. Organizing and joining protests against injustice is standing where the love of Jesus is. Participating in such protests is one way of challenging systemic racism.

A TALE OF TWO WOMEN

Murder destroys a physical human being. Rape—usually the rape of a woman by a man—damages the normal functioning of the human brain and can cause post-traumatic stress. Here is a tale of two women. In a sense each one was murdered.

She was sixteen years old on her way to becoming a major movie star. And she was absolutely gorgeous. In 1954 when she was sixteen, Natalie Wood had been invited to meet with one of the country's leading and most powerful male movie stars. She went to California's Chateau Marmot Hotel and the room where he was staying. She hoped that she would get some advice and perhaps some support for the future of her acting career. Instead, he raped her, brutally, for several hours. Natalie never told anyone, except her mother, her sister, and perhaps some very close friends. She spent years in therapy even as she continued her movie career until she tragically and mysteriously drowned in 1981.

The rape was silenced, and the name of the rapist movie star was not revealed. It remained secret for over sixty years. Finally, shortly before he died at age 101, someone in the movie industry named him—Kirk Douglas. But this was never confirmed.

A traumatic rape, which was not silenced, occurred more recently in Belgrade, Serbia. A *New York Times* article says that the face of Danijela Stajnfeld "graced billboards" in Belgrade. She appeared regularly in Serbian movies, magazines, and television shows. Trained at the prestigious Faculty of Dramatic Arts in Belgrade, Danijela had, by the age of twenty-six in 2011, won two major theater prizes and was a permanent member with the esteemed Belgrade Drama Theater.

Then she abruptly and mysteriously dropped from public view. It wasn't until the summer of 2020 that she revealed why. She had been raped by fellow actor Branislav Lecic, an older man with a prestigious reputation. She fled to the United States, broke down, had panic attacks, and considered suicide. She went into therapy and sought help in victim support groups. Then, as part of her recovery, she began to interview rape victims—and also perpetrators—for a ten-minute documentary. After three and a half years, this is a full-length movie, *Hold Me Right*. The movie had its initial U.S.

screening at the Manhattan Film Festival on June 25 and 27, 2021.[15] As of today, November 12, 2021, I have not found the entire movie released online or in theaters, but a trailer gives some idea about the film.[16]

Between the 1954 rape of Natalie Wood and that of Danijela Stajnfeld in 2012, the second phase of the women's rights movement had begun and grew. The first phase began in the 1790s with the publication of *A Vindication of the Rights of Women*, by British philosopher Mary Wollstonecraft,[17] and continued with heavy involvement in the abolitionist movement in the mid-nineteenth century. It culminated in 1920 with the 19th Amendment to the Constitution that established a woman's right to vote.

Then, on June 30, 1966, the National Organization of Women was founded, with Betty Friedan as its first president. Friedan had written the blockbuster book *The Feminine Mystique* in 1963.[18] In it she addressed the widespread unhappiness of post-World War II women being confined to the role of housewife. The "feminine mystique" was a culturally dominant idea, often portrayed in women's magazines, that women were naturally fulfilled by devoting their lives to being housewives and mothers. In contrast, Friedan's book argued that women could find meaning and fulfillment in the workplace, alongside of men.

In 1970, NOW began to address the problem of sexual violence against women. The issue is presented in the 1970 statement of purpose of the Chicago Women Against Rape: "Rape violently reflects the sexism in a society where power is unequally distributed between women and men, black and white, poor and rich. . . . In rape, the woman is not a sexual being but a vulnerable piece of public property; the man does not violate society's norms so much as take them to a logical conclusion."[19]

It was statements like this, followed by public action, that provided the background for Stajmfeld creating the documentary that grew out of her own rape. Twenty-six years earlier, Natalie Wood's cultural environment made it next to impossible for her to reveal her trauma.

Think of this, after twelve thousand years of human history (since the agricultural revolution), a dramatic shift in female-male relationships toward equality of opportunity began about fifty years ago—in the lifetimes of many of us.

---

15. See Buckley, "Her Film on Sex Assault."
16. One may view the trailer at https://www.holdmerightfilm.com.
17. Wollstonecraft, *Vindication of the Rights of Woman*.
18. Friedan, *Feminine Mystique*.
19. Schecter, *Women and Male Violence*, 35.

JOINING LARGER MOVEMENTS

In 1923, Ralph Harlow became a professor of religion at Smith College, Northampton, Massachusets. Also, following the teachings of the "social gospel," he was involved in the Civil Rights Movement.[20] When my wife Marj attended Smith in the 1950s, Harlow taught all his courses two days of the week. The rest of the week he took a bus south to help support civil rights for blacks. After he returned, he taught for another two days before heading south again—week after week. What inspired him to do this? I think the answer lies in the words of a hymn he composed in 1931, still sung in churches. Here are three verses.

> 1. O young and fearless Prophet
> of ancient Galilee,
> thy life is still a summons
> to serve humanity;
> to make our thoughts and actions
> less prone to please the crowd,
> to stand with humble courage
> for truth with hearts uncowed.
>
> 2. Stir up in us a protest
> against our greed for wealth,
> while others starve with hunger
> and plead for work and health;
> where homes with little children
> cry out for lack of bread,
> who live their years sore burdened
> beneath a gloomy dread.
>
> 3. Create in us the splendor
> that dawns when hearts are kind.
> that knows not race or color
> as boundaries of mind;
> that learns to value beauty,
> in heart, or brain, or soul,
> and longs to bind God's children
> into one perfect whole.[21]

20. The social gospel was a late nineteenth and early twentieth-century movement that put Christian social ethics into practice to address social and economic issues in society. See *Wikipedia*, s.v. "Social Gospel," last modified March 13, 2022, https://en.wikipedia.org/wiki/Social_Gospel.

21. Harlow, "Young and Foolish Prophet."

This kind of thinking and acting—even beyond the church—comes forward from Jesus's inspiring example. It is stated in Abelard's moral exemplar theory of atonement.

LOVE, JUSTICE, AND TECHNOLOGY—THE INTERNET

However, I *wonder* how can an eighty-two-year-old man with severe arthritis and a difficult time walking without falling, participate in movements that protest and work to reduce or eliminate systemic racism, sexism, and speciesism? I can't physically do something on site. However, I and others who are homebound or have work obligations can engage in activities like the following: Yesterday, I received one of many emails I get each day asking for a monetary donation to a worthy cause. Then this email gave me another option: "If you can't donate money, please share this on Facebook or Twitter." *Ah!* In addition to financial giving, or writing letters, or making phone calls to government legislators, I can share the information on the internet along with my own remarks. I remember the power of the internet during the "Arab Spring." Regardless of the final outcomes in different Middle Eastern countries, the internet provided dissidents fighting for justice ways of communicating, coordinating, and publicizing to the wider world what they were attempting and accomplishing.

As an example, I posted on my Facebook page a report about one woman overcoming sexism in her country. A *New York Times* article described how sixty-two-year-old Yayi Bayoum Diouf challenged the patriarchy of Senegal to become the first woman to engage in commercial fishing. She then encouraged dozens of women to expand their lives beyond the home—to set up hair and clothing shops, and establish other businesses such as making soap and makeup. All were supported with microfinancing from government and nonprofit sources. Then in 2015, "she used a grant from UN Women Senegal to build a farm for growing mussels, providing work for about 100 women."[22]

So, one way a local church or any other community can make a difference is for a group in the church to organize and decide what reports and actions against racism, sexism, and speciesism to post. They might begin as a "connection circle," exploring from their experience and their parts-within how each one feels about racism, sexism, and speciesism. Then twice a month, for example, they could post a story or essay on their Facebook pages or some other popular internet medium. The group could be small,

22. See "About UN Women," https://africa.unwomen.org/en/about-us/about-un-women.

say six to ten people. Perhaps there could be several groups from the congregation organized by an "outreach committee." I can see myself participating in regular Zoom meetings with other church members to decide posts. In this way a local organization can become global by using the latest internet technology. And can initiate a process of atonement, following Abelard.

LOVING GOD

A Problem of Complexity

When I began teaching environmental ethics at Rollins College in the early 1970s, there was a focus on humans overpopulating the planet. After reading *The Population Bomb*, by Paul Erlich, written in 1970, many were convinced that we would grow beyond the "carrying capacity" of earth.[23] The planet could not sustain us. More important was the increased standard of living in the United States and other developed countries. One estimate was that, on average, each citizen of the United States was using twelve times the earth's resources as a citizen of a developing country like Senegal.

In 1973, the population of our country was 216 million people. If one multiplied the number of people by the amount of resources each used compared to developing countries (12 x 216 million), we US citizens would equal 2,554,000,000 people. In 1973, the population of the world was 7,846,000,000 people. So, at that time the United States was drawing on 32 percent of the earth's carrying capacity. It was obvious to my students and me that it was completely impossible for everyone to have the same material standard of living as citizens of the United States. Clearly, we Americans had to reduce our consumption. But how could decisions to reduce our standard of living be made?

In 1973 we were still in the cold war with fearful expectations of a possible nuclear attack. At that time, a final decision to launch a nuclear attack involved only a few people, really only the leaders of the United States and the Soviet Union. However, a decision to reduce the standard of living in 1973 would require some kind of effort by almost every citizen, 212,000,000 of us. And this continues even today. Especially in a democracy, everyone has to be encouraged to reduce their draw on the planet by altering their own self-interests. Could followers of Jesus be open to the transformation of some of their own interests? Could we live as loving neighbors to earth as a whole? Could we be the "light of the world," a "city on a hill" (Matt 5:14) for all inhabitants of earth?

23. See Erlich, *Population Bomb*.

Almost fifty years later the situation is much worse. "The U.S. population is expected to grow from 333 million in 2021 to 404 million by 2060. One way to quantify environmental impacts is by estimating how many Earths would be needed to sustain the global population if everyone lived a particular lifestyle. One study estimates that it would take 5 Earths to support the human population if everyone's consumption patterns was similar to the average American."[24]

Furthermore, the problem of complexity has dramatically increased in difficulty with a myriad of technological inventions for manufacturing, domestic help, and entertainment. Even churches are using up-to-date audio-visual equipment to livestream worship services. One result of the use of more manufactured products, with both production and consumption increasing our energy use and our gaseous and solid wastes, is that we are facing climate change like never before in the past ten thousand years! We are learning that the multitude of systems involved in the workings of our planet are so interactive with one another that almost anything we do, even if successful, will make little immediate difference. Aquatic, land-based, economic, political, technological, educational, and value systems are so intertwined and constantly changing that it's easy to crawl under a blanket of fear and anger, and to numb ourselves with food and alcohol and video streaming.

It's easier to tackle problems limited to a few humans. We can tend our gardens, our workshops, our mechanical devices, even our own health and beauty. We can converse with one another about what we, our pets, and our families are doing on Facebook, Twitter, and Instagram. We can educate ourselves with excerpted books from *Blink*.[25] And I, myself, can read more mysteries. Even the systemic problems of racism and sexism are easier to grasp and work against than is climate change.

LOVING GOD

However, there may be a way forward though this complexity. Let's return to Jesus's response to the young lawyer's question, "What must I do to inherit eternal life?" Jesus said to him, "What is written in the law? What do you read there?" The lawyer answered, "You shall love the Lord your God with all your heart, and with all your soul, and with all your strength, and with all your mind; and your neighbor as yourself." And he said to him, "You have given the right answer; do this, and you will live."

24. UMCSS, "U.S. Environmental Footprint Factsheet," para. 1.

25. See the Blinkist website, https://www.blinkist.com/.

In chapter 7, we looked at what it might mean to love oneself and to love one's neighbor using ideas from psychotherapy, social analysis, and how you and I evolved into being over 13.8 billion years. Because of our common origin, all things are interrelated and, like family members, all should be loved. However, on planet earth today, because the dynamic interactions between already created living and nonliving systems are so complexly intertwined, addressing a global problem like climate change seems almost impossible. Even thinking we can solve the global problem of climate change involves hubris. It elevates us above our evolved capabilities, even with our rapidly advancing technologies.

Besides complexity, there is another fact that hinders our willingness to address climate change. We've become emotionally attached to our lives as they have been, to what has been created. There are two reasons for this attachment. First, we know well that which has already been created—spouse, children, home, car, town, business, the current economic system, and so on. Second, these have become part of our identity. The thought of radically changing *who* we are, in order to become part of a new ecologically just and caring civilization, can generate a sense of impending loss that manifests itself in grief. We grieve the death of those things that make us who we are—acquiring more material possessions, gaining more power as the leader of a business, practicing a religion that appeals to God to care for us, or following an already created set of ideas as to what a future ecological civilization might be. All these—lifestyle, power, religion, ideas about the future—are *created* goods. But because they help define who we are in ways that have become familiar and comfortable for us, we fear their loss. We grieve at the thought of needing to be re-formed in a process of transformation that is leading to a future that cannot now be very well known.

However, created goods cannot demand our total commitment. This is because they change. As the Buddha taught, all things are transient. The only thing permanent is change itself. This means that the primary way forward is to follow the first of the great commandments: "You shall love the Lord your God with all your heart, and with all your soul, and with all your mind, and with all your strength." Love God completely and consistently. This was what was required of the ancient Hebrews as they fled from Egypt and trekked—sometimes balking—toward an unknown but promised land.

From the times of the Bible and the Middle Ages, loving God for many has meant to worship and bow down before the Lord in prayer and for some to enter religious orders or occupations. However, as I discussed in chapter 2, both the Exodus and the worship of God personally, usually described as Father or King, suggest that God is thought of as a Being. This being is thought of as the source and controller of all things. But how does the Source and Controller actually work? From contemporary science and technology we have learned how many of the systems work on earth. But to causally connect the working of earth systems to a personal view of God, of what creates and sustains the world, is difficult if not impossible to establish.

However, if we think of God as the creativity of the universe—a way in which the further interactions of what has been created can work—we discard hubris and overcome demoralization as we further commit to interacting processes like those that have been creating the universe, our solar system, our planet, and us for billions of years.

LOVING CREATIVITY WITH OUR SELF AND PARTS

We have seen how creativity evolves right along with what has been created. Today, what form of creativity can we engage in that is appropriate to our humanity?

When I was in the joint PhD program at Columbia University and Union Seminary in New York in the late 1960s, I had concluded that I was an atheist. I was an atheist because I could not see how a personal God, addressed in worship as a being, could be experienced working in the world. It felt rather peculiar working toward my PhD in religion while I was an atheist.

In the second year of my doctoral program, I took a seminar from Daniel Day Williams on modern religious thought. Each student chose one thinker to study and report on from a list Williams provided. I chose Charles Sanders Peirce—considered to be the "founder" of American Pragmatism. Peirce was a scientist and a philosopher. He suggested that the *meaning* of an abstract idea consists of the experiences to which the idea points. "When he said that the whole meaning of a (clear) conception consists in the entire set of its practical consequences, he had in mind that a meaningful conception must have some sort of experiential 'cash value,' must somehow be capable of being related to some sort of collection of possible empirical observations under specifiable conditions."[26]

While I reflected on Peirce's pragmatism, I often spent late afternoons at a neighbor's apartment. There I waited for my wife, Carol, to arrive home from work. My neighbors had two daughters, ages one and three. Once, while mother was preparing dinner, the three-year-old ran up to her, threw her little arms around her mother's legs, and yelled, "I love you, Mommy! I love you, Mommy." I realized that a word like *love* could be partly defined by the action and experience of hugging.

26. Burch, "Charles Sanders Peirce," para. 27.

About the same time another friend, who had very few material goods and was struggling to keep her life together, would sometimes say, "Grace happened to me today." I had never heard this before and wondered what she meant. After several weeks of paying attention to the occasions when she used the word *grace*, I concluded that she used the word whenever something good happened to her beyond her control. Grace was a kind of event, and my friend, without realizing it, had defined this abstract concept in terms of the concrete experiences she had, just like Peirce would.

I took these experiences and, in terms of Peirce's pragmatism, wrote a short paper called "Pragmatism, Definitions, and God." I suggested that God could be thought of as a kind of event—the "grace-type event." And I further defined *grace-type event*, as "the experience of something good happening beyond our control."

LOVING THE GOD EVENT

God is an event. God is a process. God is the creative event, the creative process. God is creativity. These all point to the same thing.

Wieman helps us develop this understanding further at the human level. For "God" he also uses the phrase "Creative Interchange"—an idea of creativity that is very appropriate for human interactions. Imagine you and I are in a conversation with someone in politics or religion who is diametrically opposite to us. This was the situation of black musician Daryl Davis when he began and continued a conversation with Roger Kelly, the Imperial Wizard of the Maryland Ku Klux Clan.[27]

As Davis describes it in his TEDx talk, the encounter really began with an event that happened when he was ten. He lived in Belmont, Massachusetts, and had joined the cub scouts. He was the only black scout. In a parade from Lexington to Concord, commemorating Paul Revere's ride, his teacher asked him to carry the flag. During the parade a small group of whites threw bottles, cans, and trash at him. He had no idea why. For the first time, his parents told him, he had experienced racism. But a question formed in his mind: "How can you hate me when you don't even know me?"

Some years later, still with this question, he invited Roger Kelly to a meeting in a motel room. Kelly came with his bodyguard and was surprised to see a black man. But he stayed and they had a satisfying conversation. After more meetings, Davis invited Kelly to his house. And Kelly invited Davis to a Klan meeting. Although they didn't agree, they continued their relationship. A few years later, when Kelly left the clan, he gave Davis his robes.

27. Davis, "Why I, as a Black Man."

Fig. 37. Creative Interchange 1: Roger Kelly and Daryl Davis.
Permission granted by Daryl Davis.

In his TEDx talk, Davis points out that ignorance breeds fear, fear breeds hatred, and hatred breeds destruction. Even though they strongly disagreed, Davis and Kelly learned from one another, each taking in their differences, and they came to understand one another better. Most important, they came to have respect for one another.

Even though the descriptive language is different, I think this is an example of Wieman's creative interchange or creative event. Wieman's description is more abstract and structured, but it portrays that in which Davis and Kelly were participating. The creative event has four subevents. The first "subevent" is taking into your mind from your opposing partner some things that you don't agree with. He or she does the same. This was what Davis and Kelly did.

Of course, some of our parts are very upset because the new information creates a tension, contradiction, or conflict with what we have firmly thought. This brings us to the second step: absorb and wrestle with what your partner has given you. This usually is done in moments of solitude as we wrestle (in part subconsciously) in listening love. Eventually our thinking becomes reorganized, and we find that it is possible to combine some elements of these different views together.

A good example of combining different viewpoints is described by Cassie Jaye in her TEDx talk "Meeting the Enemy." Jaye's talk was based on her documentary, which she began expecting to support the view that men were misogynists. The goal of her new film was to "expose the dark underbelly of the men's rights movement," to "continue fighting for women's equality by exposing those most opposed to it."[28]

Fig. 38. Creative Interchange 2: Cassie Jaye and Warren Ferrall.
Permission granted by Cassie Jaye.

Jaye spent one year crossing the United States, interviewing Men's Rights Activists (MRA), including Warren Farrell, who is acknowledged to be the founder of the MRA.[29] The interviews were two to eight hours each. She recorded one hundred hours of footage, and she discovered that her initial feeling of being offended was not merited, and that it was possible to engage in open conversation. For example, it was a common theme among feminists in 2000 that men were lying when they said they were being abused. However, Jaye learned that they were not lying, not trying to play down the abuse of women, or defund women's shelters. What they were saying is that men can be abused, too, that they also deserve shelter, care, and compassion. The facts are that "about 1 in 4 women and nearly 1 in 10 men have experienced contact sexual violence, physical violence, and/ or stalking by an intimate partner during their lifetime and reported some form of IPV (Intimate Partner Violence) related impact." And "over 43 million women and 38 million men have experienced psychological aggression by an intimate partner in their lifetime."[30]

28. See Jaye, "Meeting the Enemy."

29. *Wikipedia*, s.v. "Warren Farrell," last modified January 24, 2022, https:// en.wikipedia.org/wiki/Warren_Farrell.

30. CDC, "Preventing Intimate Partner Violence," paras. 8, 9.

The two-hour-long documentary Jay created was released for the public in October 2016. It is called *The Red Pill*. This metaphor comes from a scene in the movie *The Matrix*, which offers a choice between learning the harsh and difficult truth of reality by taking the red pill, or taking the blue pill and remaining in the confining comfort generated by the Matrix, without fear and wanting nothing.[31]

Jaye says she discovered the immense value of listening to the men of the MRM. She says that all the men she interviewed supported women's rights. But they wonder why there isn't similar support for men's rights. "The greatest challenge I faced was peeling back the layers of my own bias." I did meet my enemy; it was my own ego. "We have to stop expecting to be offended, and we have to be open to truly listening."[32]

When this happens, we reach Wieman's third stage—the widening of community—and fourth stage—the deepening of community. We may even reach these stages if we don't completely resolve the differences between us. We still feel like something has happened in our interchange; we may feel greater understanding of the other, greater respect and empathy for the other, greater peace at continuing to be with the other. And so, we might continue engaging in the phases of creativity, engaging in God.

Now here's something interesting! Remember how in chapter 1 we thought about creativity and what is created as two ways of looking at the same thing. This was because what has been created becomes part of further creativity. By thinking about God as creativity or creative event in which we use listening love with others and with ourselves, we find that loving God *encompasses* loving our neighbor and loving ourselves. Because of the way humans have evolved with acting, feeling, thinking brains, we can bring a central—perhaps the central—idea and practice of Christianity into focus. *In terms of the two great commandments, when we engage in listening love with an opposing partner—our neighbor—and then when we engage in listening love with ourselves—*with our parts as they are led by self—we transcend the internalized differences. When we do these activities, *we are loving Creativity. We are loving God with all our heart, and soul, and mind, and strength.* In this love, as we engage in creativity, we more effectively address problems like racism, sexism and speciesism. We practice Christianity, following Jesus into the world.

31. The movie reflects Plato's "Allegory of the Cave."
32. Jaye, "Meeting the Enemy."

LISTENING LOVE AND FEAR

A major obstacle to people loving creativity (God) is that they are afraid to leave whatever they have—their created goods—and journey into the unknown. Even though one can argue philosophically that creativity is more fundamental than what has been created, there still is the problem of emotional attachment to what has been created for two reasons. First, we know what has already been created—spouse, children, home, car, town, business, the current economic system, and so on. They are familiar, and we are for the most part comfortable with them. Second, these created goods have become part of our identity. The thought of radically changing who we are in order to become part of a non-racist, non-sexist, ecological civilization can generate a tremendous sense of loss that manifests itself in great grief. What we fear is the death of those things that shape who we are—acquiring more material possessions in a consumerist lifestyle, having power as the leader of a business even when it exploits the planet to make a profit for stockholders, committing to a religion that assures us that God will take care of everything, or projecting an already created set of ideas as to what an ecological civilization might be like. All these—lifestyle, power, religion, ideas about the future—are created goods. Because they help define who we are in ways that are familiar to and comfortable for us, we fear their loss. We grieve at the thought of their needing to be re-formed in a process of transformation that is leading to a future that cannot now be fully known.

However, not being willing to give up created good is sin. In a dynamic relational understanding of the world and God, humans sin by tenaciously holding on to what we already have—especially attitudes and actions that threaten others, that are racist, sexist, and treat other species, ecosystems, and earth itself only as resources for our benefit. These attitudes and actions violate not only human beings and our planet. They attempt to control (or even dominate) creativity itself. So does attempting to be creative only to get human desired ends—created goods. Attempting to limit the interactive complexity—creative good—of our planet is far beyond our capacity. It works against us if we are not open to its power and scope. This is especially true of our current situation of climate change.

Yet, if we open ourselves first and foremost to creativity, if we remain open-minded, and if we are willing to experiment not only with a variety of ways of transforming the world but also with allowing ourselves to be transformed, the future may be hopeful.

TRANSFORMING THE FUTURE—WHAT HUMANS CREATIVELY CAN DO

Here are two examples in which I believe engaging in creativity has taken place. First, Bangladesh is one of the lowest-lying inhabited areas on the planet. Sea-level rise has negatively impacted the historic raising of chickens. Shopna Akter used to raise chickens while her husband worked as a laborer on rice paddies nearby. But sudden floods caused rice crops and chickens to perish and incomes to plummet. So, the couple switched and began raising ducks, a business that is now prospering. The reason for their success? "Ducks can swim." The Akters are part of a duck-farming program introduced by a local NGO that is trying to help farmers adapt to changing weather conditions.[33]

The second example is developing new energy technology for billions of people without electricity. Sub-Saharan Africa is the darkest part of the planet. By 2018, even though twenty million Africans had electricity, there were still about 595 million without access. Much of the increase has been due to grid connections, but there also has been a rapid rise in solar home systems.[34]

Small-scale rooftop solar may be a large part of the future in both developed and developing countries. A few years ago, I installed solar power on my garage roof. It now provides about 70 percent of my electricity. In *Drawdown, the Most Comprehensive Plan Ever Proposed to Reverse Global Warming*,[35] rooftop solar ranks tenth out of eighty ways to alter the climate for an ecological civilization. Here are the other nine, ranked according to amount of CO_2 created, net cost, and net savings: (1) refrigeration (removing refrigerants so they don't get into the air); (2) onshore wind turbines; (3) reduced food waste; (4) a plant rich diet; (5) tropical forests; (6) educating girls; (7) family planning; (8) solar farms; and (9) silvopasture (combining forage, livestock, and trees).[36] Note that 3, 4, 6, and 7 are not technological innovations but are lifestyle changes. Everyone can begin to do them—right now.

Being an effective partner engaging in creativity does not have to involve large-scale technologies, even though it can. Echoing E. F. Schumacher's "small is beautiful," small-scale technology like rooftop solar panels or reducing food waste may be just as effective.

We have been on a long, long journey. A journey of 13.8 billion years. The journey has had numerous significant turning points where existing

33. Savage, "To Survive in a Wetter World."

34. See IEA, "Africa Energy Outlook 2019."

35. Hawken, *Drawdown*.

36. Cornellsmallfarms, "What Is Silvopasture?"

systems were modified or destroyed, only to become part of the emergence of new systems. Atoms gathered by gravity became stars. Massive stars exploded and died, thereby creating more physical-chemical elements. Elements and atoms coalesced to create more stars, some with planetary systems. Some of these systems had the capacity to create and evolve life, intelligence, culture, technology, and civilization.

Now, in the twenty-first century, we humans have considerable power to affect how the future will be. Yet, with all our power we can only dimly see the future—or perhaps a variety of futures. And so much of what we do has unforeseen and unintended consequences. What can we do? (1) Have *appreciative love* for all that has been created, especially all our human and nonhuman neighbors who are really our relatives. (2) Seek *justice* for all who are disabled and impoverished by those humans who seek their own satisfaction at the expense of others. (3) Be ready to let go, to grieve old treasures, especially human-created treasures. (4) Most important, *love* God, God who makes all things new, God experienced as the continuous interacting between what has been created resulting in the further creation of surprising new realities. Be grateful for all that has been created, but love Creativity itself with all our souls and hearts and minds and strength.

9

AFTER DEATH

AT THE RECEPTION AFTER the memorial service for my dear wife, Marj Davis, someone came up to me and said, "Don't worry; you'll see her again," as she glanced upward. I was offended, shocked at such a selfish viewpoint. Even though she probably thought she was consoling me, her individualistic, self-centered understanding of life after death went against everything I had come to affirm.

In this chapter I'll examine, first, why belief in afterlife has been important for many. The "why question" is answered by one word, "justice." Justice means just deserts—rewards and punishments—for how one has lived his or her life. The second thing I'll do is develop an understanding of afterlife that is consistent with a scientifically based naturalism. I'll suggest that meaning and purpose in our lives can be supported by the idea of social reincarnation or social resurrection—living on as influences in the lives of other people and other forms of existence on our planet, in what we might call the "earth community."

AFTERLIFE IN THE HEBREW BIBLE (CHRISTIAN OLD TESTAMENT)

When I began McCormick Seminary in 1961, I was very surprised to learn that there was almost no idea of heaven and hell in the Hebrew Bible. There was afterlife. Everyone went to Sheol (remember Sheol in the diagram of the ancient worldview in chapter 1). Sheol was a dark and dreary place. This was consistent with the burial of the dead in the ground, so that they could more easily reach the afterlife or Sheol.[1] Sheol was part of the worldview from ancient Samaria (5000 BCE) and other later empires of the Middle East; Assyrian, Babylonian, Persian, and Greek.[2]

It also was the understanding of the people of Israel. Humans did not go to heaven after death. Heaven was the abode of God and the angels. All humans after death went to Sheol. Jesus also went to Sheol after he died on the cross. We repeat this understanding when we recite the Apostles' Creed. In the middle part of the creed, churches today use either "dead" or "hell."

> He suffered under Pontius Pilate,
> was crucified, died, and was buried.
> He descended *to the dead.*
> On the third day he rose again.
> He ascended into heaven.

The Anglican Book of Common Prayer (1662) says that Jesus "descended into hell," but the Book of Common Worship (2000) says "he descended to the dead." Generally older versions of the creed use *hell*, and newer versions spoken in Protestant Churches (Lutheran, Presbyterian, Methodist, and United Church of Christ) use *dead*. However, in 2008 the Catholic Church published a new English translation of the Mass, which began to be used in 2011. It uses the word *hell*.[3]

Among Lutherans, the Missouri Synod, which is more conservative, uses *hell*, while the more liberal Evangelical Lutheran Church of America uses *dead*. Because *hell* implies a place of punishment, I think that *dead* fits better with the Near Eastern understanding of *Sheol*.

If the word *Sheol* means realm of the dead—all the dead—where does the idea of the hell of "fire and brimstone" come from? (Brimstone is burning sulphur, which smells like rotten eggs.) And why?

I think that the ideas of hell and heaven probably developed out of a cry for justice. This cry was forcefully raised in the second century BCE. By this time the Hebrews/Jews had been under foreign domination for over 550 years. First Assyria conquered the Northern Kingdom in 721 BCE. The ten tribes of the Northern Kingdom were taken into exile, and what happened to them is uncertain. This was followed by the Babylonian conquest of the southern kingdom of Judea that culminated in 586 BCE. The Babylonians

---

1. See Mark, "Burial."

2. Many world traditions have concepts involving the dead. See *Wikipedia*, s.v. "Underworld," last modified February 20, 2022, https://en.wikipedia.org/wiki/Underworld.

3. See *Wikipedia*, s.v. "Apostles' Creed," last modified March 1, 2022, https://en.wikipedia.org/wiki/Apostles%27_Creed.

destroyed the Jerusalem temple, razed the city to the ground, and carried twenty thousand people (25 percent of the population) into exile. The anguish of being conquered and taken into exile is powerfully, even cruelly expressed, in Psalm 137.

> By the rivers of Babylon—
>   there we sat down and there we wept
>   when we remembered Zion.
> On the willows there
>   we hung up our harps.
> For there our captors
>   asked us for songs,
> and our tormentors asked for mirth, saying,
>   "Sing us one of the songs of Zion!"
> How could we sing the Lord's song
>   in a foreign land?
> If I forget you, O Jerusalem,
>   let my right hand wither!
> Let my tongue cling to the roof of my mouth,
>   if I do not remember you,
> if I do not set Jerusalem
>   above my highest joy.
> Remember, O Lord, against the Ediomites
>   the day of Jerusalem's fall,
> how they said, "Tear it down! Tear it down!
>   Down to its foundations!"
> O daughter Babylon, you devastator!
>   Happy shall they be who pay you back
>   what you have done to us!
> Happy shall they be who take your little ones
>   and dash them against the rock!

In 538 BCE, when Cyrus the Great, king of Persia, conquered the Babylonians, he allowed the Jewish exiles to return to Israel. Led by Ezra and Nehemiah the temple was rebuilt. Then three waves of empires came through and took control of Israel and Jewish life—the Greek empire of Alexander the Great, the Egyptian empire of Ptolemy I, and the Seleucid Empire based in Persia. The waves of empires ended in 168 BCE. For 553 years (beginning in 721) the people of Israel had been under foreign domination. Israel had been a monarchy for only 325 years from when Saul began his rule of Israel until the Northern Kingdom was destroyed. Scholars suggest that the historical journey of the Hebrew nation began with the exodus about 1300 BCE. From then to 721 BCE is 579 years. The length of occupation was almost as long as the independent existence of the people of Israel.

The year 168 BCE was the beginning of the Maccabean revolt and the reestablishment of Israel's independence for another hundred years. Under the leadership of Judas Maccabeus, Jews recaptured the temple and reestablished worship, including lighting a menorah that burned for eight days on only one day of oil. Today this event is celebrated as Hanukkah.

However, after a hundred years, independence was lost again when the Roman general Pompey established Roman Syria in 64 BCE and then conquered Jerusalem the next year, in 63. After this, the Jews did not become an independent nation again until 1945—after Germany was defeated and the holocaust ended.

In the years before the Maccabean revolt the people of Israel were under the Seleucid Empire and the brutal rule of Antiochus Epiphanes. An officer, Apollonius, who was sent by Antiochus, invaded Jerusalem, plundered, and burned the city. Its men were butchered, women and children sold into slavery. The temple was desecrated with a statue of Zeus, and Jewish worship was abolished.

The following, very disturbing passage from 2 Maccabees describes the cruel torture, and also the expectation of justice after the resurrection. The occasion for this brutality was the attempt to compel the Jews to eat pork.

> It happened also that seven brothers and their mother were arrested and were being compelled by the king, under torture with whips and cords, to partake of unlawful swine's flesh. One of them, acting as their spokesman, said, "What do you intend to ask and learn from us? For we are ready to die rather than transgress the laws of our fathers." The king fell into a rage and gave orders that pans and caldrons be heated. These were heated immediately, and he commanded that the tongue of their spokesman be cut out and that they scalp him and cut off his hands and feet, while the rest of the brothers and the mother looked on. When he was utterly helpless, the king ordered them to take him to the fire, still breathing, and to fry him in a pan. The smoke from the pan spread widely, but the brothers and their mother encouraged one another to die nobly, saying, "The Lord God is watching over us and in truth has compassion on us, as Moses declared in his song which bore witness against the people to their faces, when he said, 'And he will have compassion on his servants.'" After the first brother had died in this way, they brought forward the second for their sport. They tore off the skin of his head with the hair, and asked him, "Will you eat

rather than have your body punished limb by limb?" He replied in the language of his fathers, and said to them, "No." Therefore, he in turn underwent tortures as the first brother had done. And when he was at his last breath, he said, "You accursed wretch, you dismiss us from this present life, but the King of the universe will raise us up to an everlasting renewal of life, because we have died for his laws." (2 Macc 7:1–9 NRSV)

The book of Daniel was also written about the same time with the same message.

At that time Michael, the great prince, the protector of your people, shall arise. There shall be a time of anguish, such as has never occurred since nations first came into existence. But at that time your people shall be delivered, everyone who is found written in the book. Many of those who sleep in the dust of the earth shall awake, some to everlasting life, and some to shame and everlasting contempt. (Dan 12:1–4 NRSV)

As I said above, the dominant idea of afterlife throughout the Hebrew Bible (Christian Old Testament) is of Sheol—the place "under the earth" where the dead live on. However, the above two passages, one in 2 Maccabees and one in Daniel, suggest resurrection. Where does this idea come from? A likely answer is that it came from Zoroastrianism, an ancient Persian religion that the Jews encountered when they were in exile.

The founder of Zoroastrianism was Zoroaster or Zarathustra. It is not certain when he lived; some suggest about 1200 BCE. His teachings were written down in a series of hymns called the *Gathas*. Whenever Zoroaster lived, at the time Israel's exile in Babylon ended, Zoroastrianism was the official religion of the Persian Empire of Cyrus the Great. It was "practiced from Greece to Egypt to north India. It influenced Judaism and Christianity with its ideas about angels, the end of the world, a final judgment, the resurrection, and heaven and hell."[4]

Most important for our discussion of justice or just deserts are Zoroastrian beliefs (1) in a primary good deity, Ahura Mazda, who is in conflict with an evil deity, Angra Maianu, (2) in divine judgment of an individual after death, (3) in an afterlife in either heaven or hell, and (4) perhaps in universal salvation at the end of time.

Because the primary god is Ahura Mazda, the creator of the universe, some scholars think that Zoroastrianism is a very early form of monotheism. However, because of the power of evil, of Angra Maianu, others regard

4. Bowker, *World Religions*, 13.

this religion as dualistic, even though Angra Maianu is not as powerful as Ahura Mazda. The entire cosmos is an ongoing battle scene between these two all-pervasive powers. Humans have free choice to choose either side, but they must face the consequences. Those who commit evil—atrocities such as the torture killings described in the story of the woman with seven sons—will be judged for their wickedness when they die. Those who do good—good thoughts, good words, and good deeds—will be rewarded with paradise.

The mechanism of rewards and punishments is that when we all die, we will have to cross the "Chinvat Bridge," the bridge of judgment. This bridge extends over a deep canyon. If we live good lives, the bridge will widen, and we will easily cross to the "House of Song"—paradise. If our lives are evil, the bridge will narrow to the point that we can no longer cross and, instead we fall into the torments of hell. Justice is served.

However, at the end of the world all the dead, whether good or evil, will be resurrected. In a final battle Ahura Mazda defeats Angra Maianu. Evil is destroyed, and a new world order is created. The punishment of the wicked after death is not an eternal punishment; those in hell are resurrected, purified in a painful refining fire, and redeemed, so that all may enjoy the new order of things. Some scholars think that Zoroastrianism is an early form of universalism. In the end, all people are "saved." Along with justice there is mercy.

It is likely that Christianity inherits from Zoroastrianism, via Judaism, the ideas of heaven and hell, resurrection, the final judgment, and the creation of a new heaven and earth. However, as these ideas came to be expressed as a response to the problem of justice in Christianity, hell becomes eternal as in Dante's *Divine Comedy*.

THE PROBLEM OF JUSTICE IN HINDUISM AND BUDDHISM

The religions of India also think of afterlife in terms of justice—just deserts for how one lives in this current life—but in quite a different way.

I remember a classroom video that began with a Hindu man saying, "I have lived millions of lifetimes." He was expressing the idea of reincarnation or the transmigration of the soul in Hinduism. Buddhism says there is no soul but still believes in reincarnation; Jainism also affirms reincarnation of the soul, but with another understanding of how it happens.

Even with different understandings of the "soul, not-soul" all three Indian religions believe that the form in which each of us is reincarnated depends on how we have lived this present life. This is the law of *karma*, an impersonal law like gravity that says we will get our just deserts. How we are born in the next life will depend on how we lived this life. If we have lived a good life, fulfilling our moral obligations, we will be born into a better next life—maybe into a higher-class family, maybe as a god or someone higher in the "scale" of possible lives. However, if we do not live a good life, we will be reborn in a lower level of human existence with a more difficult life. If we were really bad, we could be born into one of the various levels of hell. One of my best friends in Florida, in a lunch conversation, revealed that he feared his next life. He believed in *karma* and reincarnation. He said, "I have lived such a bad life, I am terrified of my coming rebirth."

Impersonal karma is like a law of justice, of just deserts. "We will reap what we sew." This can go on for countless lifetimes. It is only when we give up all attraction to people and things, and all our negative reactions to these, that we will attain release from the endless chain of rebirths. Buddhism says that when we extinguish the flames of desire (or avoidance), we will reach *nirvana*. *Nirvana* means "extinguishing the flame."

LIFE AFTER DEATH AND THE PROBLEM OF JUSTICE IN NATURALISTIC CHRISTIANITY

So far what we have presented in this chapter is not an option for a Christianity that is naturalistic. This is because everything we have just discussed assumes a worldview that is not compatible with the worldview of modern science. (Remember the three worldviews from chapter 1.) So, is there any way we can talk about our continuation after death that fits with a naturalistic worldview? I think there is.

One thing about Zoroastrian, Jewish, and Christian views of afterlife is that they speak of our individual being as if we can experience ourselves like we do here and now. Each man and woman for themselves. This seems to be the case even though Jesus proclaimed a social understanding. For Jesus, future life was to be a "kingdom," a kingdom of God. It was a transformation to a new heaven and new earth in which the two great commandments were fulfilled: Love God with all your being, and your neighbor (anyone in need) as yourself. And Paul speaks of the communities of people following Jesus as "the body of Christ" (1 Cor 12–13). Further, the cry of the Hebrew prophets and of Jesus was for justice in society, especially for those who were poor and oppressed, who were the "least of these."

How do these social understandings of what it means to be a Christian fit a concept of our continuation after we depart our current lives? I suggest we need to consider seriously the ideas of social/environmental continuation and of social resurrection (or social reincarnation).

In chapter 2, I developed the idea of God as creativity, ongoing interaction in systems as they had been created. Stars, microbes, plants, animals, or humans become part of further creativity. In chapter 3, I told my autobiographical story (yours too) beginning as an atom of hydrogen born of the "big bang," and grown through billions of years of cosmic, biological, and human cultural evolution—always interconnected. In chapter 5, I considered two theories of atonement. The substitutionary theory (Jesus died for my sins, so I could avoid hell, enter purgatory, and finally be with God) seems to be focused on each individual. To put it bluntly, it seems like a selfish theory; it's all about me. On the other hand, the moral exemplar theory is a social understanding of salvation. Jesus is an inspiring example of how to live. As we are caught up in Jesus's love, we become inspiring examples to others. It's all relational.

How this can be understood in terms of social resurrection is expressed by a distinguished biochemist and Quaker, Max Rudolf Lemberg.

> I believe that eternity does not begin after my death; it was before I came and will remain when I die. But above all it is during my life here on earth, and this is indeed the only time during which I am responsible for my contribution to it. . . . It is, I believe, untrue that what I have done during my life, however insignificant in itself, will not count from the viewpoint of eternity. What I mean is not that it will be remembered. Nobody remembers the man who split the first flint or lit the first fire. . . . Nobody remembers the first woman who spun or planted seeds. My individual unity may be remembered for a few years and that of the great man, Jesus, for thousands of years. It is not important whether my name or any special deed of mine will be remembered; it will certainly not be remembered forever. *However, what I have done, whatever it was, good or evil, has become eternal in the sense that it has become an indestructible, irremovable part and parcel of the tissue of life of humanity.* . . . Not only books or discoveries or statements but even passing acts of generosity or lack of it—anything which has influenced other persons, adult or child, belongs to the eternal realm, even a mere loving act, thought, or gesture. That I shall not survive my uniqueness of person may be a serious blow to my self-love, but the contributions of myself and millions of other persons are not in vain.[5]

5. Lemberg, "Complementarity," 373–74. I have made some deletions and modifications in Lemberg's statement, in order to make it flow more easily, while retaining its main idea.

This idea from Lemberg reminds me of a man who had cerebral palsy all his life. He crawled around his home, pushed himself in a wagon around his small town, and talked in a guttural stammer that was barely understandable. He lived with his mother for most of his life; after she died he spent the rest of his years in a nursing home. He died when he was sixty-six.

Amazingly, the funeral home was packed for his burial service. The minister spoke on the parable of the talents from the Gospel of Matthew. This parable is about people who use their gifts wisely. As I sat in the front row of the funeral chapel, I wondered how the minister was going to apply this to my uncle Arthur Peters. Dependent on others throughout the narrow circle of his life, what did he have to offer? The minister said, "Arthur Peters had one talent; he always made people feel welcome!" As I heard this, I thought how my uncle always greeted people who came to see him. He would extend his shaking, palsied hand to offer a handshake. He would give a crooked smile. And he spoke with a slurred, "Hewo, howareyou." It was a mere loving act, word, and gesture—consistently done. Lemberg suggests that in such ways we can contribute to eternity perhaps as much as some great discoveries.

What can Christian naturalists, for whom this life on earth is all there is, expect to happen after they die? We do not expect to continue as self-aware individuals. Instead, we will continue even as we were formed over 13.8 billion years. Inspired by the deep love of Jesus, living a single lifetime, we can work toward justice in a systemic way. We can work to change the systems of oppression. We can help liberate the poor and oppressed, just like Yahweh liberated the ancient Hebrews from Egypt. We can leave a legacy of good.

Is this enough? What difference can we really make for societal and planetary well-being? In redecorating the Oval Office for incoming President Obama, some of Obama's favorite quotes were woven in the boarder of a rug. One is a sentence used many times by Martin Luther King but coined in 1853 by abolitionist Unitarian minister Theodore Parker: "The arc of the moral universe is long, but it bends toward justice."[6]

We are not alone. We work for justice in interactions with others. These interactions contribute to the ongoing, divine creativity that over 13.8 billion years of evolution has brought us to this point. Life after death is not about me. It is about how I can contribute to my corner of the universe. It is about becoming a part of the arc of history as it bends toward justice. It is about following the lead of people like my Uncle Arthur—extending a welcoming smile to all I meet. It is about following Jesus.

---

6. See *Wikipedia*, s.v. "Theodore Parker," last modified December 28, 2021, https://en.wikipedia.org/wiki/Theodore_Parker.

BIBLIOGRAPHY

Abrams, Nancy Ellen. *A God That Could Be Real: Spirituality, Science, and the Future of Our Planet*. Boston: Beacon, 2015.

Alami, Aida. "Spurred by Tragedy to a Life of Female Empowerment." *New York Times*, March 12, 2021. https://www.nytimes.com/2021/03/12/world/africa/senegal-female-empowerment-diouf-fishing.html?referringSource=articleShare.

Albright, Carol, et al., eds. *Interactive World, Interactive God: The Basic Reality of Creative Interaction*. Eugene, OR: Cascade, 2017.

Alighieri, Dante. *The Divine Comedy (The Inferno, The Purgatorio, and The Paradiso)*. Translated by John Ciardi. New York: Berkley, 2003.

Angelson, Genevieve. "Good Girls Revolt Star Shares Her Sexual Harassment Story: 'I Can't Believe I Said Yes'" *Refinery29*, October 27, 2017. https://www.refinery29.com/en-us/2017/10/178388/genevieve-angelson-hollywood-sexual-harassment.

APS News. "This Month in Physics History." *APS News*, January 2009. https://www.aps.org/publications/apsnews/200901/upload/January-2009-Volume-No-18-No-1-Entire-Issue.pdf.

Aslan, Reza. *Zealot: The Life and Times of Jesus of Nazareth*. New York: Random House, 2014.

Asthma and Allergy Foundation of America (AAFA). "2020 Allergy Capitals™ Report Ranks the Most Challenging Cities in the U.S. for Allergies." *GlobeNewsWire*, March 10, 2020. https://www.globenewswire.com/en/news-release/2020/03/10/1997870/0/en/2020-Allergy-Capitals-Report-Ranks-the-Most-Challenging-Cities-in-the-U-S-for-Allergies.html.

Badcock, Christopher. "The Dark Side of Oxytocin: Oxytocin May Be an Archetypal Social Hormone, but It Can Be Anti-Social Too." *Psychology Today*, October 25, 2016. https://www.psychologytoday.com/us/blog/the-imprinted-brain/201610/the-dark-side-oxytocin.

Banks, Adelle M. "Hymn Society Tournament Reveals 'Greatest Hymn of All Time.'" *Religion News Service*, July 19, 2019. https://religionnews.com/2019/07/19/hymn-society-tournament-reveals-greatest-hymn-of-all-time/.

Barnes, Donnie. "Bible Lands Notes: Israel." http://www.biblecharts.org/biblelandnotes/Israel.pdf.

Borg, Marcus J. *Jesus: Uncovering the Life, Teachings, and Relevance of a Religious Revolutionary*. San Francisco: HarperSanFrancisco, 2006.

Bowker, John. *World Religions*. London: DK, 1997.

Boyce, D., et al. "Global Phytoplankton Decline over the Past Century." *Nature* 466 (2010) 591–96. https://doi.org/10.1038/nature09268.

Brain Snacks. "The Dark Side of Oxytocin: The Hormone of Love . . . and Racism." *YouTube* video, 3:33, posted October 19, 2019. https://www.youtube.com/watch?v=gvI6b3DqSBw.

Brock, Rita Nakashima, and Rebecca Ann Parker. *Saving Paradise: How Christianity Traded Love of This World for Crucifixion and Empire.* Boston: Beacon, 2008.

Buckley, Cara. "Her Film on Sex Assault Depicts Her Own and Fuels a #MeToo Moment." *New York Times*, March 24, 2021. https://www.nytimes.com/2021/03/24/movies/danijela-stajnfeld-hold-me-right.html.

Burch, Robert. "Charles Sanders Peirce." *Stanford Encyclopedia of Philosophy Archive.* First published June 22, 2001. Revised February 11, 2021. https://plato.stanford.edu/archives/spr2021/entries/peirce.

Calisto Monserratt. "Mary Mother of Jesus Documentary pt 1." *YouTube* video 28:48, posted May 2, 2015. https://www.youtube.com/watch?v=DgC-oCpO9VI.

Centers for Disease Control and Prevention (CDC). "Preventing Intimate Partner Violence." November 2, 2021. https://www.cdc.gov/violenceprevention/intimate partnerviolence/fastfact.html.

Chaisson, Eric. *Epic of Evolution.* New York: Columbia University Press, 2006.

———. "Our Cosmic Heritage." *Zygon: Journal of Religion and Science* 23 (December 1988) 469–79.

Coffey, Jerry. "What Causes Wind?" *Universe Today*, December 10, 2010. https://www.universetoday.com/82329/what-causes-wind/#google_vignette.

Cornellsmallfarms. "1—What Is Silvopasture?" *YouTube* video, 2:37, posted July 31, 2018. https://www.youtube.com/watch?v=3Fqb6rT3AxU.

Corrington, Robert. "Robert C. Neville and the Great Ontological Creative Act." *Ecstatic Naturalism* (blog), January 24, 2019. https://ecstaticnaturalism.org/f/robert-c-neville-and-the-great-ontological-creative-act.

Cultural Landscape. 2011. https://culturallandscape.wordpress.com/2011/01/02/trees-of-life/.

Damasio, Antonio. "Neural Basis of Emotions." *Scholarpedia* 6 (2011) 1804. http://www.scholarpedia.org/article/Neural_basis_of_emotions.

Davis, Daryl. "Why I, as a Black Man, Attend KKK Rallies." TEDxNaperville, November 2017. https://www.ted.com/talks/daryl_davis_why_i_as_a_black_man_attend_kkk_rallies/transcript?language=en.

Denchak, Melissa. "Flint Water Crisis: Everything You Need to Know." NRDC, November 8, 2018. https://www.nrdc.org/stories/flint-water-crisis-everything-you-need-know.

Desbordes, Gaëlle, et al. "Effects of Mindful-Attention and Compassion Meditation Training on Amygdala Response to Emotional Stimuli in an Ordinary, Non-Meditative State." *Frontiers in Human Neuroscience*, November 1, 2012. https://www.frontiersin.org/articles/10.3389/fnhum.2012.00292/full.

De Waal, Frans. "Morally Evolved: Primate Social Instincts, Human Morality, and the Rise and Fall of 'Veneer Theory.'" In *Primates and Philosophers: How Morality Evolved*, edited by Stephen Macedo and Josiah Ober, 1–79. Princeton, NJ: Princeton University Press, 2016.

Diamond, Jared. *Guns, Germs, and Steel.* New York: Norton, 1997.

Elvladyman. "Before the Flood Full Movie National Geographic." *YouTube* video, 1:35:33, posted May 24, 2019. https://www.youtube.com/watch?v=zbEnOYtsXHA.

Environmental Protection Agency (EPA). "Understanding Global Warming Potentials." https://www.epa.gov/ghgemissions/understanding-global-warming-potentials.

Erlich, Paul. *The Population Bomb.* New York: Sierra Club, 1970.

Faculty of Science, University of Copenhagen. "Steppe Migrant Thugs Pacified by Stone Age Farming Women." *ScienceDaily*, April 4, 2017. https://www.sciencedaily.com/releases/2017/04/170404084429.htm.

Fraser, Giles. "The Story of the Virgin Birth Runs Against the Grain of Christianity." *Guardian*, December 24, 2015. https://www.theguardian.com/commentisfree/2015/dec/24/story-virgin-birth-christianity-mary-sex-femininity.

Friedan, Betty. *The Feminine Mystique.* New York: Norton, 1963.

Gilbertson, Sandra, and Barbara A. Graves. "Heart Health and Children." Chapter 4 of *Lifestyle in Heart Health and Disease*, edited by Ronald Ross Watson and Sherma Zibadi. Cambridge, MA: Academic Press, 2018.

Gimbutas, Marija. *The Living Goddesses.* Edited and supplemented by Mariam Robbins Dexter. Berkeley: University of California Press, 2001.

Gladden, Washington. "O Master, Let Me Walk with Thee." 1879. *Hymnary.Org.* https://hymnary.org/text/o_master_let_me_walk_with_thee.

Goleman, Daniel, and Richard Davidson. *Altered Traits: Science Reveals How Meditation Changes Your Mind, Brain, and Body.* New York: Avery, 2017.

Goodenough, Ursula. "Emergence: Natures Mode of Creativity." *Zygon: Journal of Religion and Science* 42 (2007) 829–943.

———. *The Sacred Depths of Nature.* New York: Oxford, 1998.

Grassie, William. *Applied Big History: A Guide for Entrepreneurs, Investors, and Other Living Things.* N.p.: Independently published, 2018.

Greenberg, Jon. "10 Examples That Prove White Privilege Exists in Every Aspect Imaginable." *Yes*, July 24, 2017. https://www.yesmagazine.org/social-justice/2017/07/24/10-examples-that-prove-white-privilege-exists-in-every-aspect-imaginable.

Hanh, Thich Nhat. *Living Buddha, Living Christ.* New York: Riverhead, 1997.

Harlow, S. Ralph. "O Young and Fearless Prophet." Hymn #669 in *Chalice Hymnal.* St. Louis: Chalice, 1995.

Hawken, Paul, ed. *Drawdown: The Most Comprehensive Plan Ever Proposed to Reverse Global Warming.* New York: Penguin, 2017.

Heber, Reginald. "Holy, Holy, Holy, Lord God Almighty." Hymn #4 in *Chalice Hymnal.* St. Louis, Chalice, 1995.

Helmenstine, Anne Marie. "What Is a Cladogram? Definition and Examples." *ThoughtCo*, August 28, 2020. https://www.thoughtco.com/cladogram-definition-and-examples-4778452.

Hershey, Joshua. *Faithful Science: A Christian's Guide to the Study of Creation.* Westport, CT: Libraries Unlimited, 2008.

Holland, Brynn. "The 'Father of Modern Gynecology' Performed Shocking Experiments on Enslaved Women." *History.com.* August 29, 2017. Updated December 4, 2018. https://www.history.com/news/the-father-of-modern-gynecology-performed-shocking-experiments-on-slaves.

Holstein, Alice. "Listening as a Sacred Art." Presentation, Unitarian Universalist Fellowship, February 14, 2016.

Hudry, B., et al. "Molecular Insights into the Origin of the Hox-TALE Patterning System." *eLife* 3 (2014) e01939. doi: 10.7554/eLife.01939.

Hutchings, Dawn. "Pregnant with Possibility: Was Mary a Virgin or Was Mary Raped?" *Progressive Christianity*, December 1, 2014. https://progressivechristianity.org/resources/pregnant-with-possibility-was-mary-a-virgin-or-was-mary-raped/.

International Energy Agency (IEA). "Africa Energy Outlook 2019: World Energy Outlook Special Report." https://www.iea.org/reports/africa-energy-outlook-2019.

Ireland, Perrin, and Brian Palmer. "The Full Picture of Our Lead Problem." *NRDC*, April 25, 2016. https://www.nrdc.org/stories/full-picture-our-lead-problem.

Jaye, Cassie. "Meeting the Enemy: A Feminist Comes to Terms with the Men's Rights Movement." *YouTube* video, 14:47, posted October 18, 2017. TEDxMarin. https://www.youtube.com/watch?v=3WMuzhQXJoY.

———, dir. *The Red Pill*. Documentary. San Anselmo, CA: Jaye Bird Productions, 2016.

Johnson, Eric Michael. "Raising Darwin's Consciousness: Sarah Blaffer Hrdy on the Evolutionary Lessons of Motherhood." *Scientific American*, March 16, 2012. https://blogs.scientificamerican.com/primate-diaries/raising-darwins-consciousness-sarah-blaffer-hrdy-on-the-evolutionary-lessons-of-motherhood.

Kaldas, Samuel. "Descartes versus Cudworth: On the Moral Worth of Animals." *Philosophy Now* 108 (June/July 2015) 28–31. https://www.pdcnet.org/philnow/content/philnow_2015_0108_0028_0031.

Kasting, James F., and Janet L Siefert. "Life and the Evolution of Earth's Atmosphere." *Science* 296 (2002) 1066–68. doi: 10.1126/science.1071184.

Kaufman, Gordon D. *Theology for a Nuclear Age*. Philadelphia: Westminster, 1985.

Kazantzakis, Nikos. *Report to Greco*. Translated by P. A. Bien. New York: Simon & Schuster, 1965.

Kerr, Hugh T. *Readings in Christian Thought*. 2nd ed. Nashville: Abingdon, 1990.

Kranzberg, Melvin, and Michael T. Hannan. "History of the Organization of Work." *Britannica.com.* https://www.britannica.com/topic/history-of-work-organization-648000.

Krim, Arthur. Review of *The Horse, the Wheel and Language: How Bronze-Age Riders from the Eurasian Steppes Shaped the Modern World*, by David Anthony. *Geographical Review* 98 (2008) 571–73.

Lefky, Adam, and Tamara Tamazasvili. "Number of Televisions in the US." In *The Physics Factbook: An Encyclopedia of Scientific Essays*, edited by Glenn Elert, n.p. Brooklyn, NY: Midwood High, 2007. https://hypertextbook.com/facts/2007/TamaraTamazashvili.shtml.

Lemberg, Max Rudolf. "The Complementarity of Religion and Science: A Trialogue." *Zygon: Journal of Religion and Science* 14 (December 1979) 349–75. https://doi.org/10.1111/j.1467-9744.1979.tb00369.x.

Leopold, Aldo. *A Sand County Almanac and Sketches Here and There*. New York: Oxford University Press, 1949.

Long, Charles H. *Alpha: The Myths of Creation*. Chico, CA: Scholars, 1963.

Longrich, Nick. "Did a Burning Oil Spill Wipe Out the Dinosaurs?" *The Conversation*, July 14, 2016. https://theconversation.com/did-a-burning-oil-spill-wipe-out-the-dinosaurs-62456.

Mark, Joshua A. "Burial." *World History Encyclopedia*. September 2, 2009. https://www.ancient.eu/burial/.

Mayo Clinic Staff. "Placenta: How It Works, What's Normal." https://www.mayoclinic. org/healthy-lifestyle/pregnancy-week-by-week/in-depth/placenta/art-20044425.

Morello, Lauren. "Phytoplankton Population Drops 40 Percent since 1950." *Scientific American*, July 29, 2010. https://www.scientificamerican.com/article/ phytoplankton-population/.

Morgan, Jennifer. *Born with a Bang: The Universe Tells Our Cosmic Story*. Illustrated by Dana Lynne Andersen. Nevada City, CA: Dawn, 2002.

———. *From Lava to Life: The Universe Tells Our Earth Story*. Illustrated by Dana Lynne Andersen. Nevada City, CA: Dawn, 2003.

———. *Mammals Who Morph: The Universe Tells Our Evolution Story*. Illustrated by Dana Lynne Andersen. Nevada City, CA: Dawn, 2006.

Moser, Bob. "The Reckoning of Morris Dees and the Southern Poverty Law Center." *New Yorker*, March 21, 2019. https://www.newyorker.com/news/news-desk/the-reckoning-of-morris-dees-and-the-southern-poverty-law-center.

Moyers, Bill. "Onondaga Nation Elder on the Sacredness of Mother Earth." *Vimeo* video 3:46, posted October 2, 2013. https://vimeo.com/76004072.

NASA Science. "Our Sun: In Depth." https://solarsystem.nasa.gov/solar-system/sun/ in-depth/.

Peters, Ted. "Models of Atonement." Pacific Lutheran Theological School. December 10, 2005. https://www.plts.edu/faculty-staff/documents/ite_models_atonement. pdf.

Plato. "The Allegory of the Cave." Translated by Shawn Eyer. https://scholar.harvard. edu/files/seyer/files/plato_republic_514b-518d_allegory-of-the-cave.pdf.

Plato, "Republic," Encyclopedia Britannica.

Rival Nations. "One of Many Virgins Births." *Rival Nations*. https://www.rivalnations. org/many-virgin-births/.

Robertson, Lara. "5 Examples of Everyday Sexism and How to Respond to Them." *Future Women*. https://futurewomen.com/hotlists/5-examples-everyday-sexism/.

Rolston, Holmes. *Environmental Ethics: Duties to and Values in the Natural World*. Philadelphia: Temple University Press, 1988.

Savage, Susannah. "To Survive in a Wetter World, Raise Ducks, Not Chickens." *Atlantic*, July 13, 2019. https://www.theatlantic.com/international/archive/2019/07/ bangladesh-climate-change-floods-ducks/593581/.

Schecter, Susan. *Women and Male Violence: The Visions and Struggle of the Battered Women's Movement*. Boston: South End, 1982.

Schwartz, Richard. "The Larger Self: Discovering the Core within Our Multiplicity." *Psychotherapy Networker*, May/June 2004. https://www.psychotherapynetworker. org/magazine/article/800/the-larger-self.

Siliezar, Juan. "The Cataclysm That Killed the Dinosaurs." *Harvard Gazette*, February 15, 2021. https://news.harvard.edu/gazette/story/2021/02/new-theory-behind-asteroid-that-killed-the-dinosaurs/.

Sissons, Clare. "What Is the Average Percentage of Water in the Human Body?" *Medical News Today*, May 27, 2020. https://www.medicalnewstoday.com/articles/what-percentage-of-the-human-body-is-water.

Solly, Meilan. "158 Resources to Understand Racism in America." *Smithsonian Magazine*, June 4, 2020. https://www.smithsonianmag.com/history/158-resources -understanding-systemic-racism-america-180975029/.

Strauss, Bob. "Evolution of the First Mammals." *ThoughtCo*, October 16, 2021. https://www.thoughtco.com/the-first-mammals-1093311.

Strom, Caleb. "How a Handful of Yamnaya Culture Nomads Became the Fathers of Europe." *Ancient Origins*, June 6, 2019. https://www.ancient-origins.net/ancient-places-europe/yamnaya-culture-0012105.

Sullivan, Richard E. "Charlemagne." *Britannica.com*. Last updated March 7, 2022. https://www.britannica.com/biography/Charlemagne.

Tabor, James. "A Historical Historical [*sic*] Look at the Birth of Jesus (Part 5: Conclusion)." *TaborBlog*, December 24, 2017. https://jamestabor.com/a-historical-historical-look-at-the-birth-of-jesus-part-5-conclusion/.

———. "The 'Jesus: Son of Panthera' Traditions." *TaborBlog*, January 27, 2016. https://jamestabor.com/the-jesus-son-of-panthera-traditions/.

Tebaldi, C., et al. "Extreme Sea Levels at Different Global Warming Levels." *Nature Climate Change* 11 (2021) 746–51. https://doi.org/10.1038/s41558-021-01127-1.

Tuhus, Melinda. "High Rate of Asthma for Hartford Children." *New York Times*, August 20, 2000. https://www.nytimes.com/2000/08/20/nyregion/high-rate-of-asthma-for-hartford-children.html.

University of Michigan, Center for Sustainable Systems (UMCSS). "U.S. Environmental Footprint." Factsheet. https://css.umich.edu/sites/default/files/U.S.%20Environmental%20Footprint_CSS08-08_e2021.pdf.

Wall, Mike. "Cosmic Anniversary: 'Big Bang Echo' Discovered 50 Years Ago Today." *Space.com*, May 20, 2014. https://www.space.com/25945-cosmic-microwave-background-discovery-50th-anniversary.html.

Warren, Karen J. "The Power and the Promise of Ecological Feminism." *Environmental Ethics* 12 (1990) 125–46.

Watson, W. H. *Encyclopedia of Human Behavior*. 2nd ed. Oxford, UK: Elsevier, 2012.

Wieman, Henry Nelson. *The Source of Human Good*. Carbondale: Southern Illinois University Press, 1946.

Wollstonecraft, Mary. *A Vindication of the Rights of Woman*. 1792. Reprint, Mineola, NY: Dover, 1996.

Yglesias, Matthew. "Swarthy Germans." *Atlantic*, February 4, 2008. https://www.theatlantic.com/politics/archive/2008/02/swarthy-germans/48324/.

Zalesky, Carol. "Purgatory: Roman Catholicism." *Britannica.com*. https://www.britannica.com/topic/purgatory-Roman-Catholicism.

Zimmer, Carl. "DNA Deciphers Roots of Modern Europeans." *New York Times*, June 10, 2015. https://www.nytimes.com/2015/06/16/science/dna-deciphers-roots-of-modern-europeans.html.

———. "A History of the Iberian Peninsula, as Told by Its Skeletons." *New York Times*, March 14, 2019. https://www.nytimes.com/2019/03/14/science/iberia-prehistory-dna.html.